PLAN YOUR ROUTE

PLAN YOUR ROUTE

THE NEW APPROACH TO MAP READING
(Including the electronic technology
and satellite navigation)

Victor Selwyn

DAVID & CHARLES
Newton Abbot   London   North Pomfret (Vt)

USE OF MASCULINE THIRD PERSON PRONOUN

In this book the map reader or navigator is referred to as '*he*' and what happens will be to '*him*' as '*he*' finds '*his*' way. I could have written throughout – 'he/she', 'him/her', 'his/her', as the book applies to all taking part in map reading and route finding – but this would only clutter the text.

British Library Cataloguing in Publication Data

Selwyn, Victor
    Plan your route: the new approach to
    map reading: including the electronic
    technology and satellite navigation.
    1. Maps
    I. Title
    912'.01'4   GA151

    ISBN 0-7153-8892-4

Diagrams in Parts 1 to 6 are based on originals by Jack Partridge.
The book derives from my first manuscript entitled *Common Sense Map Reading* (see Dedication).
Some of the methodology and diagrams from that manuscript have been used elsewhere without acknowledgement. However, the original manuscript bears the stamp and date of GHQ, MEF, with permission to publish.

Typeset by Typesetters (Birmingham) Ltd
and printed in Great Britain
by Billings Ltd, Worcester
for David & Charles Publishers plc
Brunel House   Newton Abbot   Devon

Published in the United States of America
by David & Charles Inc
North Pomfret   Vermont 05053   USA

Contents

Acknowledgements

The author gratefully acknowledges the help, advice, comparing of notes and inter-change of ideas with Lt. Col. (Ret'd) Ben Burrows, author of the Ministry of Defence Manual on Map Reading and the staff of the School of Military Survey, Hermitage, Berks: Brigadier Hugh Woodrow (ex-Ordnance Survey), Professor Stuart Sutherland, Head of Experimental Psychology, University of Sussex. The help from the Ordnance Survey, the Automobile Association and Royal Automobile Club in Britain is greatly appreciated AND the most generous help from the Automobile Association of America, Stuart B. Hopkins, William C. Sunier, Chief Cartographers, and the United States Geological Survey. The permission from George Philip & Son Ltd., to use Lt. Col. Lockey's 'Classification of Land Forms' is acknowledged. Also permission acknowledged from Lt. Col. Ben Burrows on material in Part Eight 'The New Technology'. I thank my colleague, Dr rer.pol. Christoph Seidelmann, of the Studiengesellschaft für den kombinierten Verkehr eV., (Institute of Combined Transport Studies) Frankfurt, for information on technical developments in Germany, and thank scientists at the Road Transport & Research Laboratory in the U.K. The reproduction of material from the Ordnance Survey (Maps A and B), John Bartholomew and Son, American Automobile Association (TRIPTIK), Automobile Association (Map C) and RAC and Michelin, with their permission.

Finally, thanks to my old friend Jack Partridge, who drew many of the original diagrams in a tent in the Desert, including Diagram 16, and undoubtedly thanks to R.S.M. Sid Glazier of the East Surrey Regiment – he could see round corners – who first asked me to instruct on map reading. He began it all.

To Whom This Book is Directed

This book is written for *all* interested in map reading and route finding, whether civilian or military. Whilst covering the subjects one expects in a book with *map reading* in its title, this book goes further in two respects:

  (i) it is concerned with the *use* of the map in the wider subject of route finding, navigation.
 (ii) it is directed to the world in a hurry, to those on wheels, having to make decisions at speed, as well as to those who use a map on foot.

For this book is for those who walk *and* for those on two wheels or four, or on tracks across country, on both sides of the Atlantic. It includes desert and mountains.

It is an *instructional* book, too. It follows in principle the course of a specialist map-reading and navigational instruction unit, directed by the author.

Hence the same subject, developed in different settings, especially that of *direction*, a major element of route following. This also reinforces learning. Hence, too, the series of exercises in the book whereby the reader derives the full benefit from the text.

SEQUENCE OF SUBJECTS IN THIS BOOK

Inevitably in the sequence of principles, theory and then application, there will be an overlap of subject matter. However, the book aims to present the subject in a logical progression.

Part 1 summarises the elements of route finding. Here is spelled out the basic rules, the do's and don'ts, however you travel – on foot, on wheels, on tracks across country or desert, by day or by night. This statement of principles precedes the *reading* of the map in Part 2. How to *use* the map in the field, along with the compass and protractor fits into Part 3, which returns to route finding, its planning and following, in more detail. Part 4 becomes mobile – on wheels, or tracks; the problems of decision at speed. References are appended to Part 4 on psychological studies relevant to the methodology of this book. These methods are applied to the desert and on the mountains in Parts 5 and 6. Desert navigation, incidentally, does not only concern vast expanses of sand and scrub. The techniques extend to similar areas, short on landmarks and features that can be identified for sure on the map. Part 7 deals separately with the USA.

Part 8 looks forward to the technology of the 21st Century where the application of electronics to land navigation is introduced.

Appendix A comprises a series of exercises to help the reader master the subject. There is also a note on instruction.

Appendix B concerns memory.

Appendix C outlines Field Sketching and panorama.

Appendix D illustrates dead reckoning as applied to Desert Navigation.

Notes on Terminology

This book has been written for readers on both sides of the Atlantic. However, the usage of certain words and phrases differ. A *crossroads* in Britain becomes an *intersection* in the USA. In Britain one *turns* right, in the USA one *makes* a right.

A *motorway* in Britain, a purpose built road for motor vehicles only with limited access, can be a *freeway, expressway, parkway*, in the USA. In France such a road would be an *autoroute*, in Italy, *autostrada*, in Germany, *autobahn*.

In general this book uses the words and phrases current in Britain, especially as regards *motorways*, an omnibus word to cover this type of highway. Otherwise it would be necessary to write again and again, *motorways/freeways/expressways/parkways*.

Of course, the special section on the United States uses the American terms.

This book is dedicated to Sir Peter Scott, CBE, DSC. Hon Chairman of the Council of World Wildlife Fund International, whose spirit of exploration of the world around us must inspire any navigator and user of maps.

By coincidence there is another Peter Scott whom I must recognise – a Captain, who taught survival and navigation at Combined Ops HQ, Lochailort, Scotland, all those years ago in World War II. For his concept – contours, the backbone of the countryside – and other dicta that so neatly fitted into the book, entitled *Common Sense Map Reading*, I was writing then and once again fit into this book produced in the era of electronic technology – I thank him.

Introduction

The use of electronics in navigation is not new. Without it planes would not land and take off at the intervals of a bus service, or giant tankers navigate busy shipping lanes or sail into port.

But a map with a moving arrow on a VDU in a car, and a synthesised voice to tell which way to go is new. There are difficulties that will be explained in this book. Even so, it is possible to predict that fleets of cars will be equipped with electronic navigation devices announcing 'turn left or right 100 metres ahead.' This being so, will the need to master the map and understand navigation vanish like the use of a starting handle on a car? If this were so, then an aircraft would not need a navigator with his maps, or a ship an officer in a chart room.

The automated car route finder will not end the headache of the indifferent map reader. A poor navigator will need more than a magic box. For the technology has to be programmed, followed and changed, if need be, en route. To choose the software you need to know maps. *You have to make decisions.* The machine to do this is not in a box at the back of the car. It resides in your head, a machine more complex and flexible than any computer, the human brain.

The brain is the prime instrument of all navigation, whatever help is to hand. Successful route finding, on wheels, on foot, on tracks across country or desert, turns on its use in observation, in learning, in memory and, above all, **commonsense.**

Commonsense, the use of one's wits, has nothing to do with academic brilliance. On the contrary many geniuses lack everyday wisdom – and, interestingly, are poor route finders. For commonsense turns on a recognition of realities, of cause and effect. If we do 'A' then 'B' will happen – not 'C' instead, as the expert, wrapped in his theory, will predict. In any case that expert will probably have seen a *different* 'A'. It is the ability to see what is and not what should or might be that underlies commonsense.

True, the expert will sell himself successfully, though not on successful predictions, but on image. Image would not take you far in finding your way, especially in the world where the methodology of this book was born, that of mobile war – no signposts; no lights at night; no 'phone box to dive into to ask one's way; split second decisions on the move and a penalty for mistakes. The lessons learned there, both in instruction and in the field, apply to the widest range of route finding problems; from those anxious to get off the motorway at the right exit to the lost climber on the mountainside. The book considers these problems among many others.

First, one lesson, gained in instruction and observation of would-be map readers of differing abilities. It reads as an apparent contradiction but it certainly held and will hold, for it deals with human behaviour:

> Those who dither without a map, and have no notion how to set about finding their way, will usually do little better with a map, sometimes even worse. The best map reader, it will be found, is one who needs a map least. That can hold for any navigation aid. Hence the earlier prediction on the new technology.

This basic proposition underlines the approach of this book. For the map enjoys no inner magic that will lead willy-nilly to where you want to go. The subject you need to master is route finding, planning and following a route. A map is part of it. But first learn the basics of navigation. It is this approach that differentiates this book from others.

Let me illustrate this thesis in three scenarios.

Problem 1: You are on a motorway and ahead see a traffic block stretching to the horizon. Not an unusual sight, unfortunately. If you could only get around it! You have to decide – and decide quickly for even as you slow you may cover 15m (50ft) in a second, so in a minute you might go by a turn you could have taken. The trouble is twofold: all you know for sure is the route of the motorway – and motorways tend to insulate drivers from the world outside; secondly, there is the pressure of an appointment you must keep and you are late already. You may have a plane to catch. This adds to anxiety which impedes clear thought. What do you do?

You may even have a car equipped with an electronic compass and a system to measure accurately distance covered, a map display on a VDU (facing the passenger seat in the UK) and a panel telling the route to take. The instruction can only be *keep to the motorway*, if that is how the computer was programmed before you set out to choose the direct route and whilst you are driving you cannot safely feed new information into it, even if you need only to use a simple code to divert onto a new route.

That will have to wait until you leave the motorway or find a safe place to stop.

You can read the signs with road numbers and places. But if you follow them off the motorway, will they lead in the wrong direction? Where will you rejoin your original route? There is but a minute or more to decide and act. That is the headache of all wheeled navigation; decisions to be taken at speed, with opportunities gone whilst trying to decide. You may also be prevented from taking a side road by having to cross lanes of traffic if you leave it too late. It would be different if you could stop, but on a motorway that is out.

Problem 2: You are on a mountainside and the mist descends. The track divides. On the map are a number of forks and track junctions. But which one is this? Is it on the map at all? This is not a mountain on which one can take chances. Scree is marked. (Tracks divide in other places than on mountainsides. Anywhere across country. Can you be sure that what is seen on the ground is the junction on the map?)

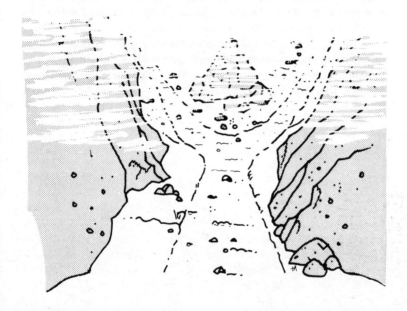

Problem 3: You are driving a truck across desert. A storm has blown soft sand across well-used tracks. You have had to divert and find it hard to relate the map to the scene in front of you. A storm or two soon makes a map out of date. Your rendezvous is a six-figure map reference in a wadi (a valley, usually dried up), so you will not see it or be seen from far off. Ahead is scrub, rocky outcrops and sand and some empty oil drums.

Examine now the three scenarios. In each case the fact that you have a map still leaves you with an unsolved problem. For more than the map is needed. You need to know route finding, a far wider subject than map reading; you also need the ability to apply your wits, calmly and rationally.

15

In **Problem 1,** you could not look at a map at all whilst driving, not even *consult* a map on a VDU, if you had one in the car. So any decision must be taken without the benefit of the map. The study of the map must happen *before* setting out and at stops en route and what you need to know from the map must extend beyond the motorway (see Part 4).

In **Problem 2,** on the mountain, you will be looking hard at the map; but the map cannot speak. It cannot tell in the conditions of little visibility precisely where you are. What is needed here is the experience and knowledge of mountains.

Problem 3 truly shows the limitation of the map. You need other aids to navigation. If you were lucky the truck would be equipped with Magnavox, that gives latitude and longitude to within a few hundred metres, which is fine in a desert as you may see your

destination from a distance. Yet even with electronics there is the problem of navigation, for although you can get a bearing on your rendezvous, you cannot drive in a straight line on that bearing. The desert takes over. It is a question of where you *can* drive. At the end you may still have to search to find the rendezvous. It is in a wadi. Crossing the desert demands *skills* which must be *acquired* (see **Part 5**).

Route finding involves a range of skills – the use of a compass and the sun and the stars; knowledge of types of country, urban layouts and road systems, aside from the ability to use a map – *and commonsense.*

Commonsense tells you:

(i) you cannot both read a map and move at speed at the same time, or even move slowly and study that map at the same time. True, orienteers run around the country with a map in hand *but* the map reading mostly takes place before one sets out, to be checked en route.

(ii) hence you must plan beforehand; marshal the essential information from the map and other sources.

(iii) any plan must be systematic and *simple*, because,
(a) in following it you depend on memory and the less to retain the better (see **Appendix B**).
(b) in an activity, that may often entail stress, the simpler route may be preferable even if longer.

(iv) a plan recognises that you are governed in what can be done, not only by your mode of travel and by time of day, but because, in general, following a route forms part of another exercise – your work; you have an appointment; even on holiday you have to get to a place on time or you may wish to see other places en route – or if military, you may be conducting a reconnaissance where tactical considerations predominate and may have to change that plan at any time.

However you move, on foot, on wheels or in a tracked vehicle, there are elements common to all route planning and following.

So organise your journey that once started you need consult the map as little as possible. Obviously no method is foolproof so tailor any system to your own ability. For navigation begins with the navigator. Route finding – and within it, map reading – is an exercise in human behaviour.

Here the beginning of wisdom is the Socratic dictum – know thyself. Some people are lucky enough to find their way with little apparent effort, as if guided by magic. Most, though, have to learn from experience, from instruction and books. Difficulties stem from the fact that homo sapiens, of the western world anyway, is not a natural navigator – streets, houses, signposts and transport direct us. Man lacks the innate ability of the bird that returns to its nest after a 4,000-mile migratory round trip. If he ever had an awareness of direction and distance, the veneer of what is called civilisation has overlaid it.

Our forebears certainly taught themselves navigation. Without this ability the Persians, the Egyptians, the Greeks and Romans could not have controlled such widely dispersed empires, nor the Phoenicians traded with Brittany and Cornwall. Fifteen hundred years and more later, mariners from the Iberian Peninsula and from England sailed small ships into unknown waters around the world.

We must marvel not only their skills but also their courage. No radio. No satellite navigation aids. No planes to rescue them if anything went wrong. No maps until they drew them. They had to do their own charting. Fortunately there is so much help to hand today; yet to use the tools of navigation effectively *it is essential first to develop one's own route finding faculties. Hence the exercises in this book.*

The basic methodology was first outlined in an instruction hand-book for an army in mobile war. As a contemporary Middle East manual put it (somewhat understated), 'The scope and scale of military movement has greatly increased.'

For now units had to operate at speed in difficult and unsign-posted terrain.

Map reading now was **'on the move'**, a contradiction in itself, for that is when a map could not be read.

So one had to go back to first principles, to identify the problem. It was one of navigation, route planning and finding. Systems were evolved to cope with speed of movement. These have now been adapted and brought up to date and also look ahead, with benefit of researches and experience in the UK and USA and on the Continent of Europe.

In recent years, the researches of experimental psychologists have tended to confirm methods derived from experience, obser-vation of human behaviour and commonsense (references listed in Part 4, Section 12).

I have compared notes with and sought advice from the School of Military Survey in the UK, especially on the new technology, and have consulted the AA in Britain as well as the American

Automobile Association with its staff of more than forty carto-graphers at its Fairfax County HQ (near Washington DC), who bring maps up to date and deal with problems of members making two- and three-thousand-mile trips across the USA, only to be lost in the last ten or twenty miles, when they get off the main highway. One place looks like another and what are called streets may run for miles, then disappear into the woods to reappear on the other side (acknowledgements are listed in **Appendix D**).

This introduction concludes with advice to the reader:

(i) the approach of this book is pragmatic. If it works in the experience of those advising and writing this book and especially those, instructed and observed, it is in. If not, it is out. The reader must be pragmatic, too. Methods are not to be applied blindly but adapted to situations and to *one's own ability and experience*.

(ii) to benefit from this book, the exercises should be undertaken at the stage where they appear in the text (some are partly repeated in **Appendix B** on memory). These exercises are designed to make you aware of the subject, appreciate the points made. In this, you teach yourself; *who better?*

SUSSEX, GT. BRITAIN.
1987

Part 1
The Approach to Route Finding

Section 1: Introduction

However proficient anyone may be, in all route finding it is necessary to be systematic. Begin with a check list before setting out. This check list forms the base line of this book.

1 Define objective of journey. Mode of travel. On foot/on wheels/on tracks. *How important is time?* By day or by night? Do you want a scenic route? Quiet route? The motorway? If military, tactical considerations – cover.
2 On your own or with other people and/or vehicles?
3 Have you the *correct* map or maps for the area?
4 How well do you know the area through which you will travel?
(a) the shape and layout of the country – the natural features?
(b) the manmade features? Towns and road systems?
(c) the main directions, to build into a 'directional framework' of which you can memorise and relate places to?
(d) key distances?
5 Can you identify landmarks, prominent places, distinctive features by which to fix your route?
6 Now relate time and distance.
7 Note decision points, possible trouble spots, where you may go wrong, where to take special care.

Section 2: The Do's and Don'ts *(Try first Exercise 1)*

A sequence of places, way points, will describe a route. Where the route presents changes and/or choice there will be decision points. However to ensure the described *route is followed this book presents the concept of* identification *points, recognisable places that may also serve as landmarks. Landmarks of course identify and locate the key points en route and may even lie off the route.*

The Three Basics
A route instruction comprises three factors:

   (i) identification points/landmarks; (ii) direction; (iii) distance

Call establishing them the *do's* of navigation; now what you must *not* do, two *don'ts*.

(i) do not plan by counting of turnings. No *second* on the left, followed by *third* on the right. 'Second on the left' on the map may *not* be 'second on the left' on the *ground*. A map selects. The slip road you see ahead – is it on your map? This means forgetting the habits of a lifetime, acquired in the built-up world where one thinks in a sequence of turnings, 'second on the left' or 'third on the right'. This habit helps least when you depend on a map of limited scale in an unknown area.

(ii) as for 'left' and 'right', this is the next habit to overcome. When you plan, think out a route; do *not* use *left* or *right* for directions. Use bearings, the points of a compass, North or South, East or West and so on. The world outside works this way. True, when you drive along you will *turn* left or right, or instruct someone to do so. But the plan is thought out – and retained – in North, South and so on. It saves you going wrong, *especially in open country*, and in urban areas, too; to be *aware* of directions you must *think* in bearings or points of the compass. Establish the directions of main features this way. Incidentally, also learn directions of city and urban roads and streets, which is easy in New York though less so in Birmingham, England. The key here is to establish a framework of main streets (see **Exercise 5**).

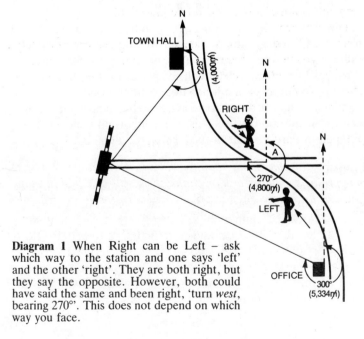

Diagram 1 When Right can be Left – ask which way to the station and one says 'left' and the other 'right'. They are both right, but they say the opposite. However, both could have said the same and been right, 'turn *west*, bearing 270°'. This does not depend on which way you face.

21

Always associate a direction with a main street name. Aside from the fact that some people confuse left and right, especially under stress, as any drill sergeant or driving instructor knows, left and right *depend* on which way one faces. North and South do not. Your 'right' can be someone else's 'left' (see **Diagram 1**).

Examine the three elements of the route plan: landmarks, direction and distance.

Landmarks

Landmarks that locate the route:

(i) give the places that can be identified for certain – confirming you are on the right route. Hence a suitable landmark will have some unique quality in relation to its neighbourhood. A golf course may be fine but there may be more than one in that area, as are electricity power lines.

(ii) will be on the map unless, of course, you can add local knowledge when guiding someone else, eg turn North at the Lion Hotel.

(iii) a landmark must be recognisable at the time you expect to be passing – experience will teach you, for instance, the features you can recognise at night.

(iv) the contours on a map can establish a landmark, eg the end of a long descent, especially at night and better in conjunction with distance recorded on the car's mileometer*, to make sure.

Landmarks may lie away from your route; prominent features you can see from the road or track you are following; a line of hills, parallel to your route. The turn you want may come 5km after the end of that line. Be wary, though, of places on that line of hills, such as a promontory; one looks like another.

Landmarks may also anticipate action to be taken some distance ahead as on the motorway. This is an important concept that is developed in Part 4 – that of *anticipatory* landmarks.

Direction

Just as landmarks *with distance* replace the counting of turnings, the bearings on a compass replace left and right. All bearings are measured clockwise from a line running North, 0°. Then at 90°, is East, 180° South, 270° West and so to 360°, the full circle. North East is 45°, South East, 135° and so on (see **Diagram 1A**).

The army works in mils, 6,400 mils to the full circle instead of 360°. 1,600mils, East, 3,200mils South, 4,800mils West. Mils are shown as m̷ (m with a stroke through it) or on German maps with a

---

*See later note on mileometers under Distance.

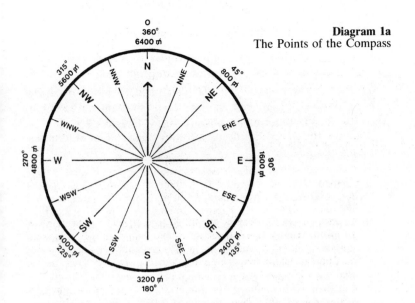

dash, eg 1,600m mils. Mils were introduced for the artillery. The navy and air force still use degrees.

Everyday awareness of direction by the points of the compass is certainly needed for road signs and highway reports. When highway reporters announce a 5-mile tailback of *westbound* traffic on the M4 or congestions of *southbound* traffic on the San Diego Freeway, there can be no dispute as to which lanes of traffic are afflicted. (For the problem of directions and motorway inter-changes see Part 4. I shall deal with bearings and the problems which arise in more detail in Parts 2 and 3.)

Distance
Distance forms the third element of route planning. Any plan must include distance from point to point. This may be labouring the obvious, but distance is especially needed when there are no land-marks, as on many motorways or in the desert, or in any feature-less country where one operates by dead reckoning. You log the journey, the direction and distance from the last reference point and so establish, you trust, where you are (see Part 3). Your turn point may be 72km (45 miles) from a landmark and so at 69km (42 miles) you begin to look out. Your ability to do so depends on the accuracy of your car's mileometer, a most neglected tool of route following. However, many are inaccurate. All depend on correct tyre pressures and even if accurate, are not easily visible as you drive. It pays to invest in a supplementary trip recorder, clearly

23

visible by day or night, that can be set at zero at the start of a journey (see Part 8 for the electronic solution).

Whether on foot or on wheels, you need to judge distance, without continual reference to a map. To do this you must think in *time* as well as kilometres or miles (try now **Exercise 2**).

    (i) on foot one can average 5km (3 miles) an hour in a steady march. But across broken country you may be lucky to average 3km. In the hills one has to add at least half an hour for each 300m, (1,000ft) climbed. Difficult terrain has a time of its own, including the desert. Obviously, when conditions are difficult distance covered and time tend to be exaggerated. So you should practise; add time for 400m across a field to 300m through a copse. Judgement of distance provides the first check on the route. If after travelling 3km, 40 minutes, across open country you should have reached a river and no water is in sight – and, even worse, you are going up hill – then something is very wrong. On wheels, the map indicates that 30km (18½ miles), 25–30 minutes, after a main highway intersection you should be passing an airfield and there is no sign of it, then maybe you took the wrong turning – or the map is out of date, although even a disused airfield remains visible. On the positive side, time and distance will locate turn points on the highway.

   (ii) on wheels *the stops* add up. A Ferrari takes the same time in a traffic block as a Volkswagen Beetle – longer maybe than a bicycle!

  (iii) on a motorway or freeway it makes no sense to say you can average 88km or 55 miles in an hour or more, just because that is the legal limit. Motor roads can get very crowded and foggy and are constantly under repair. Even under favourable conditions to average 88kph, you need to reach more than 110kph (70mph) for stretches of the route if there is other traffic on the road. Before dawn it may be different. You also have to allow for time in and out of cities and built-up areas. Cross-country routes can average 50km in the hour (31¼mph). But sometimes with clearer roads and less traffic than the motorway you may well increase that average. This is where the map comes into its own.

  (iv) at night one tends to underestimate the passage of time. On foot, especially, distance traversed may be overestimated. There isn't a day timetable of getting up, work, meals, and so to bed, against which to relate the hours. Time is underestimated even more when one is engrossed in another activity, as infantry on patrol at night can testify. The last look at the watch showed 1am; now it is 3am. The two hours seem to have vanished. Time can be misjudged, too, in a car on a long distance trip through the night.

Finally distances on a long, straight, stretch of highway tend to be underestimated, while distances with many bends are often overestimated, as are distances in town centres as compared with the outskirts which have fewer features. Hence the instructions to draw a sketch map in **Exercise 3**. Space the distance from place to place first, then draw the road in between and include only the important bends.

(See study, *Memory for Urban Geography*, Cambridge, England, by R. W. Byrne, Dept of Psychology, University of St Andrews.)

Section 3: The Tools of Navigation*

The tools of navigation can be divided into two categories:

(i) what one has and aims to develop: the psychological factors:
observation/recognition
memory
awareness of direction
judgement of time and distance
common sense
systematic recording and use of information, knowledge of field-craft, country, urban and main road patterns.
(ii) the instruments
map
compass
protractor
electronic/computerised navigation aids
add notebook, ruler (metric) and pencils – and a sketch pad if you need to record what you have seen.

One item, only to be used carefully, is a chinagraph pencil with which to trace a route on a talc cover over a map. This method can create an illusion that the route traced on the talc is clearly defined on the ground. In reality this route only exists in the map reader's imagination. He has created it for himself with a pencil on a piece of plastic. And attempts to follow it may lead into difficulties. Often the chinagraph line obscures important features. The china-graph pencil should be used, more to *supplement* the information conveyed by the map and to pinpoint landmarks. Chinagraph route finding is certainly not recommended.

Psychological Factors
The introduction underlined the psychological factors in naviga-tion, **above all commonsense**. Previous sections dealt with judge-ment of directions of time and distance. Apparently there is a

---

*The tools of route finding will also be dealt with in more detail in other sections of this book, in their application to specific problems.

great deal to master but in fact, what you must do is to develop faculties you already have.

The key is practice. In direction, for example, when going to work, or to the pub, you must say 'I am going East or South' and then, when returning, 'West or North'.

Every day you carry out 'observation' and 'recognition'. In route finding you observe places, shape of country; details you must recognise and remember, that identify routes.

Now different people notice different aspects of the same scene. Two people watch a football match on TV. One comments on the oldfashioned shorts of the players. The other sees a central defender moving quickly into the space to receive a return pass from his colleague on the wing. What the two see depends on what interests them.

What interests the route finder is seen in the contents of this book. To observe more accurately, record the detail of journeys during and afterwards in a notebook. Do you recognise instantly the landmarks that identify the route, recognise them when you see them and recognise your destination when you get there? The latter is no academic question, particularly for the military map reader under orders to rendezvous at a reference number on a map. Can you identify the place from the map, the task dealt with in Parts 2 and 3?

Memory plays an essential part in all this (see **Appendix B**). As stressed, it is impossible to move and study the map at the same time. Ideally, the skeleton of the route should be memorised, or recorded on prompt cards (see Part 4), as well as the identifying landmarks *and* the relevant layout and shape of the country.

Before setting out to master navigation – and map reading – try finding your way around part of the country you do not know, *without* a map, compass, or any other aid, armed, of course, with a notebook to record what you do. Whenever possible try a new route to a familiar destination – again without map but with just a general idea of the direction in which to go.

Once you succeed, you gain confidence as well as knowledge and better observation. The introduction recommends a pragmatic approach – techniques not to be applied blindly and, simpler, even if at times longer, routes *if there is a commitment*. This does not mean *never* to try the difficult route. On the contrary that is how you learn. But there is one time for experimenting and another time when route finding forms part of another exercise; a destination must be reached with the least trouble especially when others are involved.

Then it is best to remember that route finding, like government is the art of the possible, though you cannot charge your mistakes to the taxpayer; you pay.

The Instruments

So to the map, to the compass and protractor. I shall deal at length with these instruments of navigation. Here is a brief description of their use to put them into context.

1 The map proves central to all route planning; its information is needed. (The map is also needed by a wide range of static users, from estate agents to locate property to generals to plan a defensive position.) Its use, of course, is limited by what the map includes and what it leaves out. For a map is a *selection*, determined both by its scale and its purpose.

2 The compass gives directions; it measures bearings from magnetic North. A sun compass is used in a desert, where direction is given by the shadow cast by the sun. This robust instrument has the advantage of not being affected by the metal of a truck or engine – and is easier to drive by.

3 A protractor measures and plots direction on a map, and is also used to locate a position en route. A lightweight compass, used by orienteers and the military, incorporates a compass with a protractor. It speeds operations. The heavier liquid prismatic compass may be used for more precise measurement, particularly at night.

4 Finally there are electronic navigation aids, products of the new technology. Their greatest value lies in giving location and direction, especially for wheeled navigation. However, for a long time they must remain expensive, incurring two sets of costs: one for the instrument, the other for the software to programme the computer. To operate one has to know the map detail needed and hence the cassettes to use for the part of the country or urban area. Obviously in operation they cannot be more accurate than the map on which they rely. Moreover to use technology effectively you must know the subject. This applies in any field. A doctor could hardly use a CT Scan without knowing medicine and know what he is looking for and interpreting what he sees.

The pages ahead will present the instruments of navigation in more detail.

Part 2
How to Read the Map

Section 1

Problem: Can you look at a map and picture reality? That is, from the map can you know what you will see from the ground, at rest, or as you walk or drive? A *sideview* is needed. From the map you could construct a model but that gives an 'over the hill' view. You are not in a balloon.

From the ground many features shape the view – and hide it, too, eg folds in the ground, buildings, even a fence. You don't always know whether they are on a map. That is the problem of the prime tool in navigation.

The map depicts an area of country on a flat surface by a series of symbols, eg for a road, river, church, forest, railway. The map not only reduces three dimensions to two – height is depicted by contours and figures – but also represents the curved surface of the Earth on a plane sheet. Like pressing out flat peel of an orange, this leads to distortion and creates problems when a map is overprinted with a grid on parallel lines. The grid must inevitably diverge from lines of longitude. The curvature of the Earth also affects intervisibility; what can be seen from one point to another (see Section 3).

The map is drawn to scale: 1in on the map represents 1 mile on the ground, or 4 miles or 10 miles. Today in Britain the scales are becoming metric, 1 to 50,000 (1cm equals 0.5km) taking over from the 1in to 1 mile, the 1 to 63,360; 1 to 250,000 (1cm equals 2.5km) formerly 4 miles to 1in map – and so on (see later section on scale).

An aerial photograph also gives a picture of an area of country. The difference between the map and the photograph lies in the map being a *selection* of features in symbol form, whereas a photograph shows all that the camera sees. In contrast the aerial photograph needs an expert to interpret it. It does not show the same scale throughout and depends on the angle from where it was taken. The photograph is affected by shadow and light.

Who then selects the features to print on the map? The answer

28

will be found in the margins around the map – or in the preliminary pages, if in a book.

Check the following:

(i) who conducted the survey on which the map is based
(ii) who is the publisher – sometimes the same as (i)
(iii) the purpose of the map, eg motoring map
(iv) the scale; for this must limit what can be included
(v) the date, not only of survey and production but also of revisions and which is most important, especially regarding roads.
(Certain military maps also carry a reliability diagram when the map is not up to expected standard.)

The maps in Britain are based on the Ordnance Survey which are indicative of their accuracy. Although maps were produced long before, the systematic surveying of Britain began during the Napoleonic Wars, in 1791, when the Ordnance Survey* began to use triangulations that have underlied all the maps until today's aerial surveys (for the USA, see Part 7).

As the maps were military in origin, the features first included were primarily of interest to the soldier on the ground; rivers, roads – fenced and unfenced (unfenced enable troops and transport to leave that road in a hurry), bridges, contours, woods, urban areas. Of course these features interest other users, too. But as will be stressed throughout this book, there may be important features the map does not show. This is the problem. For a map, like one's perception, is selective.

Whoever does the survey, in the end, in any country it is the publisher who finally determines the accuracy of the map as well as who chooses what to include.

There are variations in detail and accuracy. This can only be learnt from experience, and it pays to compare one map with another to see how they depict an area you know. The problem for all map makers is to keep their maps up to date. It costs money. In Switzerland one commercial map maker, Kümmerley + Frey, believed a rival was copying its work and so introduced deliberate mistakes in its next revision to see what its rival would do. The suspicions were confirmed. Never take anything for granted and one simple way to compare accuracy of, for instance, Continental map makers is to study the maps they produce of Britain, in whole or in part.

---

*In the 1980s in Britain the Ordnance Survey was transferred to the civilian Department of the Environment; a recognition of the wide interest and demand for maps from all sections of the community, but the techniques used derive from the Royal Engineers.

Obviously the purpose of the map affects the choice of features to include. The Ordnance Survey identifies the intended user in its present series, eg 1 to 25,000 Pathfinder Series and the Outdoor Leisure Maps for the walker,* climber, cyclist and keen tourist; 1:250,000 Routemaster for the motorist and the 1 to 50,000 Landranger Series in between intended for detailed exploration by car and on foot. Continental map makers have always specialised in maps for the tourist, marking roads and places from where one can view the scenery. The Ordnance Survey has become multilingual, and even shows picnic and camping sites as well as viewpoints.

In general, the smaller scale map for the motorist will show less than a map for a walker or mountaineer. (In a later section it will be noted that two sets of maps are used for long journeys: a smaller scale map covering a larger area on which to plan the overall route and a more detailed map for planning an intermediate or final stage. United States' users may need three or four maps.) Compare a motoring map with a larger scale OS Map and see how much some motorists' maps leave out, often omitting contours and spot heights and some railways and bridges, *which can prove useful as landmarks*. Not so the contoured Ordnance Survey 3 miles to 1in book of maps for the motorist in Britain, which is really a blown-up 1:250,000; among the best of British motoring maps and good value!

Too many motorists' maps, however, reflect the belief that the motorist needs only road information and the towns and places en route; not always enough, especially when locating landmarks to identify one's route.

Finally, on the selection of features, here is an example from the world of advertising: on hoardings a large map may show where the hotels belonging to a chain are located in that part of the country. Does the map show contours, heights, all the waterways – unless a hotel overlooks a river? The map will show just the minimum detail needed to guide the customers to the hotels.

If a hotel is opposite a railway station, then the station is shown; or by a church, in the town centre, then the church; and just the basic road system to link the places on the map. Little more than necessary is shown, although the scale may be huge. *In the end, the*

---

*Note the OS Maps to cover the Long Distance Path routes in Britain, as well as National Parks. Moreover, the distinctive marking of long distance paths and recognised rights of way.

publisher and purpose determine the selection of details on the map.
When you have to draw sketch maps you take over this rôle.
What you include turns on why you are making that map.

The Sequence: What to Look For
So the purpose of the map, scale and maker determine the features
that will be included. You learn what to expect and what is left
out. Suppose you have a map in your hands for the first time.
Summarise the points to look for. Establish a sequence. The points
are all relevant and if they seem obvious, they are all essential (see
previous section). They are included here as part of the drill.
Note:
1 The maker and the scale: note if distances and heights are in
   metric or imperial measure.*
2 Area and sheet number, ensure that the map covers the area
   you need. The title is not enough. Note the grid system.
3 *The date of last revision*; a map is soon dated.
4 The setting of a map and its grid. Do not assume the top of the
   map points North. Usually it is so – but not always. At the side
   of the map check the pointer that indicates magnetic North and
   its variation from grid and true North. The variation differs – to
   the West of true North in Europe and East of true North on the
   USA West Coast. Against magnetic north variation, *note again
   the date*, another check on when the map was printed.
5 Finally, note the key to conventional signs, the symbols that
   indicate the features the map includes. You think you know; but
   they vary and are added to. The second series of the 1:50,000
   has signs in addition to the first series. So this is the drill:
   *Map maker : scale : area sheet number : grid system : date :
   direction : conventional signs*

Section 2: The Essence of the Map

A map is a map because it is drawn to scale. Any other way of
representing an area of country should be called a sketch or
picture. The scale defines a map. A map is referred to as 1:50,000
or 1 mile to the inch. This tells the detail to expect and the purpose
for which to use that map.

---

*The Ordnance Survey in the UK has distances in both, and heights in metres, except for the
1:250,000 where heights remain in feet. This map is used by aviators as altimeters throughout
the world record in feet.

31

There are three ways of representing scale:

(i) representative fraction, eg 1:25,000 or 1:50,000 or 1:63,360
(ii) statement of fact, eg 1cm to 25,000 metres, or 1cm to 50,000 metres, or 1in to the mile
(iii) by a diagram of units and sub-units drawn at the foot or side of the map, so that one can read off simultaneously, say, 2.5cm or 1in and equate it with 1.25km or a mile.

These diagrams are termed linear map scales. A typical example is given here. To the left of zero are the sub-units and to the right the major divisions.

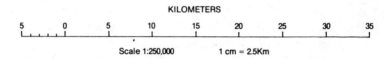

Diagram 2 Linear Scale

From the linear scale one can rapidly measure distances. With the ruler or straight edge, measure distance from one point to another on the map and then transfer the ruler to the linear map scale. This gives distance as the crow flies. If the route winds, use a thread to follow it on the map – or buy a map measurer. Try to estimate visually the length of 1, 5 or 10cm (or inches on an older map). The practice is rewarding.

Of the three ways of stating the scale, the representative fraction is the most difficult to work in when using inches for miles. A metric map has fewer headaches. Note, incidentally, *that the representative fraction holds true for any unit of measurement, inches or centimetres.*

The scale of the map determines the features you may expect to find on it. Conversely, the amount of detail which has to be shown influences the maker in choosing the scale. A route diagram covering the British Isles hardly needs a scale larger than 16 miles to the inch or 1 for 1 million, but such a map would be useless for a walk on the Sussex Downs. On the other hand, a driver from London to Scotland would find a series of 1:50,000 OS maps impossible to handle. To cross the USA a driver would need a library of maps to this scale.

To appreciate scale, examine how the same area is represented on three different maps: on 1:50,000; 1:250,000 and on a small scale map in an atlas (see **Maps A, B, C** on pages 34 and 35).

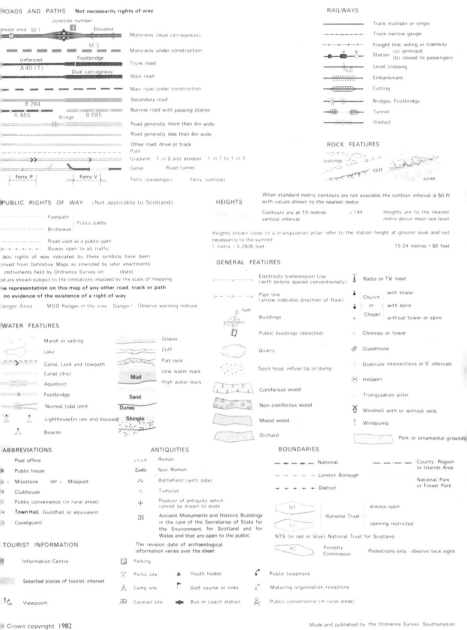

Diagram A: Ordnance Survey Conventional Signs

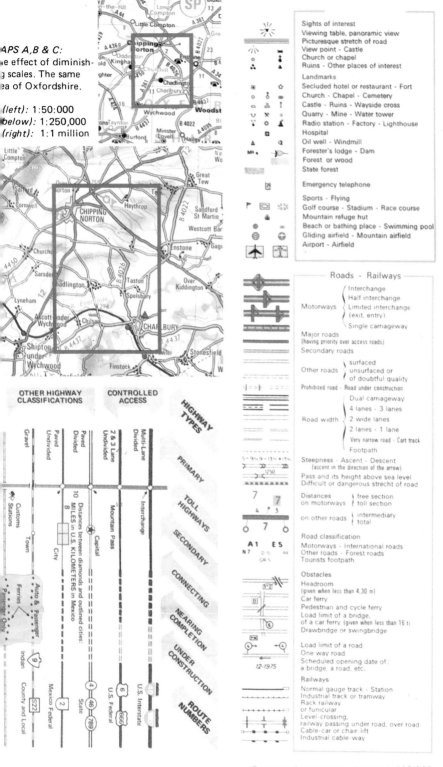

APS A, B & C:
e effect of diminish-
g scales. The same
ea of Oxfordshire.

(left): 1:50:000
(below): 1:250,000
(right): 1:1 million

Sights of interest
Viewing table, panoramic view
Picturesque stretch of road
View point - Castle
Church or chapel
Ruins - Other places of interest

Landmarks
Secluded hotel or restaurant - Fort
Church - Chapel - Cemetery
Castle - Ruins - Wayside cross
Quarry - Mine - Water tower
Radio station - Factory - Lighthouse
Hospital
Oil well - Windmill
Forester's lodge - Dam
Forest or wood
State forest

Emergency telephone

Sports - Flying
Golf course - Stadium - Race course
Mountain refuge hut
Beach or bathing place - Swimming pool
Gliding airfield - Mountain airfield
Airport - Airfield

Roads - Railways

Motorways { Interchange / Half interchange / Limited interchange (exit; entry) / Single carriageway

Major roads
(having priority over access roads)
Secondary roads

Other roads { surfaced / unsurfaced or / of doubtful quality
Prohibited road - Road under construction
Dual carriageway

Road width { 4 lanes - 3 lanes / 2 wide lanes / 2 lanes - 1 lane / Very narrow road - Cart track / Footpath

Steepness - Ascent - Descent
(ascent in the direction of the arrow)
Pass and its height above sea level
Difficult or dangerous stretch of road

Distances { free section / toll section
on motorways
on other roads { intermediary / total

Road classification
Motorways - International roads
Other roads - Forest roads
Tourists footpath

Obstacles
Headroom
(given when less than 4.30 m)
Car ferry
Pedestrian and cycle ferry
Load limit of a bridge,
of a car ferry (given when less than 16 t)
Drawbridge or swingbridge

Load limit of a road
One way road
Scheduled opening date of:
a bridge, a road, etc.

Railways
Normal gauge track - Station
Industrial track or tramway
Rack railway
or funicular
Level-crossing,
railway passing under road, over road
Cable-car or chair-lift
Industrial cable-way

OTHER HIGHWAY
CLASSIFICATIONS

CONTROLLED
ACCESS

HIGHWAY
TYPES

PRIMARY

TOLL
HIGHWAYS

SECONDARY

CONNECTING

NEARING
COMPLETION

UNDER
CONSTRUCTION

ROUTE
NUMBERS

Diagram B: AAA: USA Highway classification

Diagram C: Michelin, France 1:200,000
map Conventional Signs

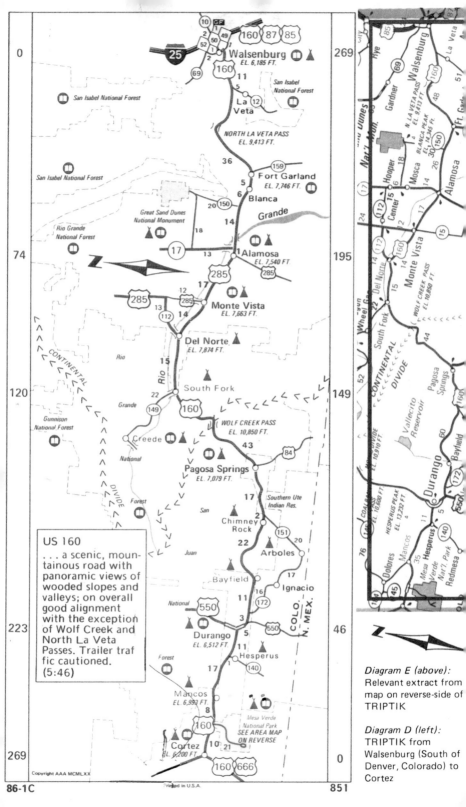

US 160

... a scenic, mountainous road with panoramic views of wooded slopes and valleys; on overall good alignment with the exception of Wolf Creek and North La Veta Passes. Trailer traffic cautioned. (5:46)

Diagram E (above): Relevant extract from map on reverse-side of TRIPTIK

Diagram D (left): TRIPTIK from Walsenburg (South of Denver, Colorado) to Cortez

86-1C

Diminish the scale, and minor features disappear. The twisting road now runs straight and may disappear altogether. Note the detail on the first map, the 1:50,000, showing the area to the East and South of Chipping Norton in Oxfordshire in Britain. Now see what has vanished on the 1:250,000 map of the same area. This latter map is more for the motorist – but see what is left in the tiny extract from the 1 to 1 million map in the AA handbook – the road network from Chipping Norton and the corresponding area to that depicted on the other two maps has become so small that it can show little more than a road or two.

This awareness of features disappearing as the scale diminishes proves vital. Now you can see why you can take a wrong turning if you try to follow a route by counting the turnings. The third turning on one map may be the first on another – or not exist at all on yet another map.

Before using a map, look at the scale and judge what it should and should not include.

Scale and Distance
Always retain the idea that *scale* represents the actual distance to be traversed. It must be automatic to look at a map, and say, 'from point A to point B is 7km'; to glance at the diagrammatic representation of the scale at the foot of the map; and to make intelligent use of the grid system.* Of course, you need to know the length of a centimetre or inch and judge these distances without having to measure them.

The next stage is to think of distances in *time*. (Refer again to elements of route finding.) Two centimetres on a 1:50,000 map means 12 to 13 minutes on foot in average country, or a minute or less in a car. Failure to relate speed with distance can result in overshot turnings or the realisation you have passed your rendezvous on the road or cross country.

Map References
Maps, especially military, can be overprinted with a grid, whereby any point can be located accurately to within 100m, for example on an OS 1:50,000 map (see footnote).

The grid is a rectangular system, usually pointing to the North at the top of the map. It may not point to true North, as the grid is

---

*See 'Map References'.

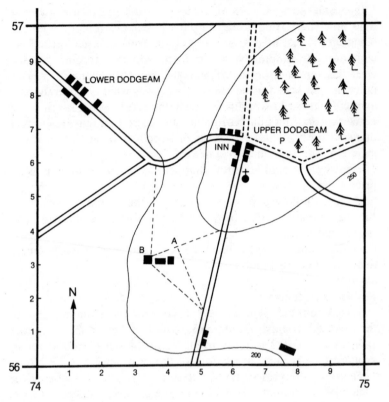

Diagram 3 Reference Numbers on Grid Square (RZ) 7456 (enlarged for purposes of illustration)

flat and is superimposed on a curved surface, that of the Earth. This does not present problems until you have to convert bearings (see later).

The grid divides the country into:

(i) 100m squares on maps of 1:10,000 or larger scales
(ii) 1km squares on 1:100,000, 1:50,000 and 1:25,000
(iii) 10km squares on smaller scale maps

Each square is identified from the South West corner by a four figure reference (see footnote for Gt Britain). Accuracy is essential in giving map references. Yet for some reason many map users have problems, mainly that of *sequence*. Two simple rules prevent mistakes. First, here is how to identify a point on a map.

38

Diagram 3 shows an area of country. If asked to rendezvous at a track junction near some farm buildings to the South of the Upper Dodgeam Road, you would first have to locate the village of Upper Dodgeam on the map, then the road referred to, then the farm buildings, and hope that you have identified the correct track junction. All this process can be easily simplified by means of a map reference which will indicate the rendezvous.

As explained, Great Britain is covered by a system of grid squares (in kilometres) based on a point to the South and West of the country, from which to imagine lines to the North and East. The distance from this base point is the map reference of any given place.*

There are two sets of grid lines, at 1km intervals; those which measure the distance to the East (74 and 75 in Diagram 1) which are termed Eastings (although these lines *point to the North*), and those which measure the distance to the North (56 and 57 in Diagram 1) which are termed Northings, (although these lines *run towards the East*). Any grid square is numbered by its south-western or bottom left hand corner, eg the grid square in diagram 1 is numbered RZ 7456 and any place in that grid square, such as the village of Upper Dodgeam, can be referred to as Upper Dodgeam 7456. 7456 is called a four figure map reference. (As explained earlier, the letters RZ are not needed.)

To be more accurate, go one stage further. Imagine the side of each grid square being divided into ten equal parts. Start on Easting 74 and go along four tenths, ie 744, then proceed with Northing 56 and go up three tenths, ie 563. This gives a combined reference 744563, which is a track junction 'A'. Here, at once, is the value of a six figure map reference; for if in the rendezvous was a track junction, you could quite easily go to the other track junction 743563 'B' – hence the necessity for accurate map references and their value in defining a position.

Note: Most of the world is covered by the Universal Transverse Mercator Grid System, called UTM, from 80° to 84° N. The UTM grid is divided into zones of 6° longitude and 8° latitude and subdivided into 100,000m squares.

Great Britain has its own Grid system based on a point to the South West of Britain (see Ordnance Survey publication *An Introduction to the Projection for Ordnance Survey maps and the National Reference System*, HMSO 1951). Each 100km square is designated by two letters. All measurements are from the South West corner.

The use of a two letter prefix is peculiar to Britain and in practice the letters in giving a map reference are dropped while working in a given area.

*Grid systems in other countries operate in the same way, viz, measured from a point to the South and West, giving Eastings and Northings.

Two Rules to Guarantee Correct Map References

Here are two rules that could not be more simple to ensure correct map reference:

1 **Right up** (Eastings – Northings).
2 **Do not** start going up until you have *finished* the *third figure of going right*.

Another way of stating the first rule is 'to the tree and up the tree'.

The second rule turns on the word 'finished'. Complete one operation before going onto the second.

Rapid Estimation of Distance by Grid Lines

On a 1:50,000 OS map, the side of a grid square is 1km long. Each tenth is therefore 100m (approx 110yd). So given two map references it is easy to determine the distances between them. Generally a quick idea of the distance may be gained by counting the grid lines crossed when working out a route on a map.

Use a romer to measure accurately within a grid square. Put the corner of the romer against the place being identified, with the edges of the romer parallel to the grid lines. Read off the distances.

Romers are included on protractors – on the military protractor RA for scales, 1:25,000, 1:50,000 and 1in to the mile. Obviously a different romer is needed for different scales. The lightweight compass and protractor also include the romer. Finally, a romer can always be made from stiff board, subdividing the grid square into tenths on two sides (see **Diagrams 4 and 5**).

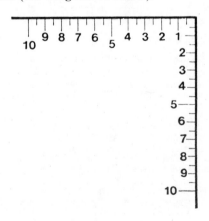

Diagram 4 Romer

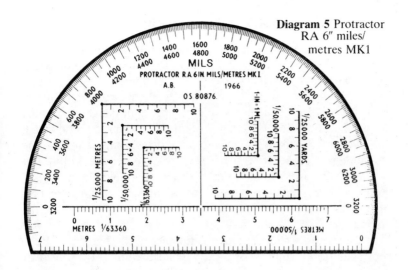

Diagram 5 Protractor RA 6″ miles/ metres MK1

For two reasons the use of geographical co-ordinates, for giving a position in latitude and longitude, may take over from grid systems in many parts of the world:

(i) there are problems with the use of a grid, especially where adjacent maps use different grids.

(ii) satellite navigation systems give positions in latitude and longitude though, of course, they can be programmed for grid if need be. However, primarily they give geodetic co-ordinates – including height (see Part 8).

Section 3: Conventional signs: the ABC of the map

The task in map reading is to build a picture of the country from the map. Look at a printed sheet. Can you see the country it represents?

(i) do you understand the signs?

(ii) know the country, its shape and layout? Is this chalk country? Clay? Limestone? The map will not necessarily tell, but it is important to know. This is dealt with in the next section.

The map maker builds his picture by means of conventional signs. An extract from the Ordnance Survey 1:50,000 second series shows conventional signs (see **Diagram A** on page 33). Another extract shows the road classification symbols of highways from the AAA map in the USA (see page 35). The identification of highways is paramount for the motorist in the USA, where one

41

operates so much by route numbers; whilst the motorist in France, using a Michelin 1:200,000, will have three signs for steep gradients, signs for a cable car, a panoramic view, a church, secluded hotel or restaurant, windmill, golf course, a load limit on a road, a one way road and even for a difficult or dangerous stretch of road (see page 35). (The cover of this book shows a section from the Michelin Normandy map; the reader can compare it with one in the Alps.)

There are no short cuts in the learning of conventional signs.* You just have to memorise them, though most are self evident and in any case you can refer to the margin of the map if in doubt (try **Exercise 6**).

In many cases the signs are commonsense. There may be a representation (symbol), or a plan or an elevation, or both plan and elevation of the object simultaneously. For instance a windmill is represented both by its side view and a line for the base. Similarly trees of various types have both a side view and a short line at the base representing a shadow.

Signs are also classified as to whether they represent:
   (i) natural features
   (ii) manmade features
   (iii) unseen, eg boundaries

Some complain that map makers have not overcome the problem of drawing boundary lines that look like tracks. This is a source of confusion as are electricity transmission lines. The best advice is to follow on the map a feature that looks like a track until one is sure that it is not a local or a national boundary. There are other signs that look alike as the inspection of the margins of the map will show.

Section 4: The Shape of the Country
Bridging the Map with Reality
To bridge the map with reality, more than the symbols on the map are needed. It is important to know the structure of the country, the type of scenery likely – and this is determined by its geology. The types of rock not only shape the scenery but also largely

---

Note: Field Sketching Signs
The military map user especially will also have to learn field sketching signs that are given in the manuals and are more on the lines of the impression various features make on the eyes of the observer. They are simple to draw. New symbols are being created constantly: though, if in doubt, any symbol would do so long as the field sketcher sticks to commonsense in designing conventional signs.

govern where people live and what will grow and what will be seen. On the map – in the following pages – are rivers and contours. But note first what underlies them, the geology.

In Britain* there are:

(i) the chalk, rounded scenery in the South East of England, with no streams on the surface and few trees
(ii) the limestone of the Cotswolds, with its typical building stones, a few streams, more trees; also in Yorkshire
(iii) the harder limestones of the Pennines with outcrops of rock and caves
(iv) the clay soils of East Anglia; flatter country, many rivers and copses
(v) sandstones, which being porous produce heathlands and open land, not worth cultivating, but fine scenery in the Weald of Kent and Sussex and in Devon
(vi) the granite of the Lake District and Pennines and Highlands of Scotland.

It pays to discover the geological pattern for any country operated in or visited.

You may not travel with a geological map but if you note the scenery you encounter and then consult a book on its geology you can soon become familiar with the types of landscape. This helps to build a picture from the map. The great teacher here is the sketching of *miniature* country. Operate with a sketch book; *miniature* country will familiarise you with the land forms.

You may be sketching clay country or limestone or granite and see that the country is made up of valleys, hills, with spurs and re-entrants (see diagram 6) and note the shape of mountains and passes and plateaux. You could go in for modelling – a hill, a valley, a spur – and the routes you take. However, a note of caution; you will not see the ground as represented by a model. **The country needs to be seen from the ground – the sideway view.** Hence the value of 'miniature country'. Sketch what you see, using elementary form lines, to indicate the shape of the country. If looking up a valley, draw the form lines indicating the surrounding higher ground and perspective of the valley. Make it simple – the basic lines to show the shape of the country. The act of sketching has an added advantage since it develops the knack of the thumbnail sketch for illustrating reports – and increases observation.

---

*I am indebted to Lt Col B. Lockey for his useful classification in *The Interpretation of Ordnance Survey Maps*. George Philip & Son.

Contours: The Backbone of the Countryside

Now to the map! The key to establishing the shape of the country lies in two sets of features – too often neglected, especially the contours.

(i) the water; (ii) height: contours and spot heights.

The sequence of study of any area on the map begins with the water, the sea, the rivers and streams. For water shows where the land is lowest. Moreover if the river winds towards its estuary then it is in very flat country, possibly intersected by drainage canals, as in the fens in England. Towards the source of the river, with streams flowing into that river, are hills, with land sloping down to the streams and river. Water is a help in landform recognition, the typical shapes of country, the change in scene as rivers leave hills and cut their way through to the plains.

Contours, spot heights and trig points tell the rest. From water and the lowest land look for spot heights, the greatest heights, and then study the contours; the guide to the shape of the country.

Contours join points of equal heights, spaced at intervals, 25ft on 1:25,000 or 50,000 on the Ordnance Survey or 200ft on the 1:250,000, formerly the Quarter Inch Map. Maps can also show height by colour; green at sea level, and shades of yellow becoming brown and darker higher up.

Although the contour lines are actually in feet on the 25,000 and 50,000 Ordnance Survey Maps, they are shown in metres, eg the 200ft line, in a darker brown, is marked 61m, and two lines above, the 250ft line, 76m. This forms part of the change to metric. The current surveying of the United Kingdom, now mainly from the air, is in metres and already on the new large scale 1:10,000 series (6.36in equals 1 mile), from which new maps at other scales will be prepared. (As stated earlier, heights on the 1:250,000 are likely to stay in feet, though, for this is the map used by aviators.)

In addition to spot heights on OS maps there are 'trig points', the latter showing from where the area was surveyed.

The contour lines tell a great deal. The closer the lines, the steeper the slope. Where contour lines are closer at the foot of the slope than higher up, there is a spur of land and conversely, a typical valley, or re-entrant between spurs of higher ground will have the contours more widely spaced in the lower reaches. Contour lines so close that they can hardly be seen apart indicate an escarpment or cliff.

44

Diagrams 6 and 7 show a typical system of a valley between two spurs from a range of hills. Note that the contours of a valley are wider apart in its lower reaches, whilst the contours of the spurs are closer together towards the foot of the slope. The latter are important as they imply 'dead' ground and one needs to be well forward to view the lower slopes.

In terms of convex and concave:

(i) where the contours are closer together at a foot of a slope than at the top of the slope is convex as with the spurs

(ii) where the contours are further apart at the foot of the slope than at the top there is a concave slope, the valley which rises more gently lower down.

To study the shape of the country, having looked at the water and then at the highest points, now take a pencil and, on tracing paper over the map, trace round the contours at certain fixed

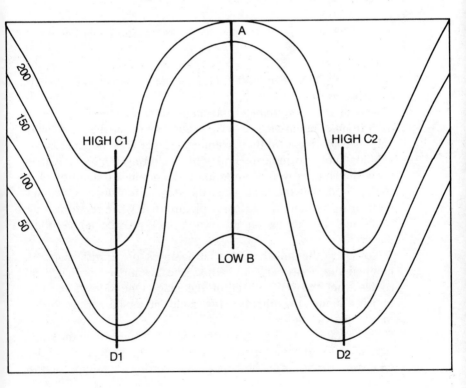

Diagram 6 Re-entrant (valley) between spurs

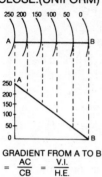

STEEP CONTOURS CLOSE.(UNIFORM)

GRADIENT FROM A TO B

$$= \frac{AC}{CB} = \frac{V.I.}{H.E.}$$

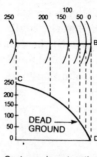

CONVEX SLOPE

Contours closer together at foot of slope. (Spurs)

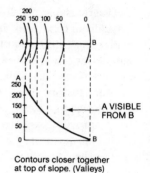

CONCAVE SLOPE

A VISIBLE FROM B

Contours closer together at top of slope. (Valleys)

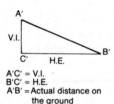

A'C' = V.I.
B'C' = H.E.
A'B' = Actual distance on the ground

Diagram 7 Shape of Slopes

intervals, eg 200ft (61m), 400ft (122m) and at intervals in between (see **Exercise 7**).

At once the main shape of the countryside will stand out. Here, as in route planning, it may pay to study first a smaller scale map with its colourings and then examine a larger scale detailed map.

Maps may also indicate slopes by hachuring (hatch lines that show shading) as well as contours or sometimes instead of contours; the darker the hachuring, the steeper the slope. Contours on their own often give a clearer picture than when reinforced by hachuring. Hachuring on its own cannot provide an accurate picture.

However, the hill-shading that features on tourist maps of mountainous areas certainly helps. The assumption is that light comes from the NW corner of the map. One side of the hill remains 'sunny', the other is in the shade and the darker the shade, the steeper the slope.

I have referred to contours as the neglected features on the map, especially for the motorist; yet contours are important to the motorist.* Apart from helping in discovering the shape of the

*See also later 'Contours as an aid to Route Finding'.

country from a map, contours may prove a guide on an otherwise featureless road and provide landmarks and, more important, anticipatory landmarks – alerting the user on what to do kilometres ahead – a point made earlier. At night the rise and fall of the road may indicate where you are. But there are limitations to the information given by contour lines, you will see in a later section. And a map does not always tell you what you can actually see from where you are on the ground. The odd hedge, line of trees or fold in the ground can obscure the view. This arises in problems of 'intervisibility'.

Further use of spot heights – trig points

Where the contour lines are printed so close together that they cannot be numbered, an odd spot-height will help to determine the heights of the adjacent contours, since no two adjacent contours can be more than one vertical interval apart. Furthermore, it can be safely assumed that the land falls away from a spot-height where the pattern of contours indicate a summit; or if the spot-height is on a road, then the road *usually* slopes downwards both ways from the spot-height. Trig points are equally useful and if a group of such points are close to each other, one may assume that one trig point is visible from the next trig point; that is how the map was originally made.

This comes to a stock question in map reading, viz, how can one tell high ground from low ground if the contours are not numbered? Again, the obvious, rivers, railways and large centres of habitation mean low ground; uncultivated areas with few man-made features usually mean higher ground. However, the answer is in the shape of the country.

Although unnumbered contours may not distinguish high ground from low ground, in normal topography various land-forms, eg valleys, have distinctive contour formations. Just study a map that includes a valley you know well. *Hence the stress on the study of landforms and miniature country.*

Limitation of Contours

In the Yorkshire Dales and in many places where a road follows a river towards the source the road, instead of climbing steadily, is more like a switchback. Yet if you consult a contoured map it would appear that the road went uniformly upwards. The reason? The river, being there first, carved a bed for itself in the lowest part of the land between the hills. Man, who followed thousands of years later, was forced to build his road over the foothills at the side of the river. The ups and downs however in the road, are only in the region of 6 to 8m (20 to 25ft) and since the vertical interval on a 1:50,000 OS map is 8m (25ft) the ups and downs of the road might be missed out altogether. Sometimes the rises and falls in the road will be shown by the same contour line crossing and recrossing the road; but not always. This is the principal limitation of contours viz, if the contour interval on a map is 30m (100ft) and the general level of the country is 90m (300ft) then elevations above the general level will **not** show as such on the contour map, unless heights go above 120m (400ft). On a plain a low knoll of 10m may prove of vital importance – yet there may be no indication of it on the map. In undulating country the folds in the ground play an important part yet, without a prior knowledge of the type of countryside, it is impossible to make a correct appreciation from the map (**Exercise 7**).

Water and Contours and other guides in Route Finding

Not only is the general configuration of the country in itself an important aid and guide to the route finder; for mountaineers and for those driving tracked vehicles across hilly country the contours may be as useful as a main road.

For instance, you can look at the map and see that if you follow a certain height, you will strike a stream whose bed leads to your destination. Many, if asked the key to successful route finding on the mountains, will answer that they try to 'keep height' (see **Diagram 30**).

The map has other useful information to help in making an appreciation of hilly country. If the road winds with many acute bends, the area is not only hilly, but there are probably drops at the side of the road. Moreover, the road does not climb uniformly; it probably dips a few times before reaching its summit and may have more bends even than the map indicates.

Look closely at a river system and you may locate a focal point for the area, maybe just a pond to which all the water drains and so the land slopes towards it. Now relate water to the contours. If contours cross a stream or river at close intervals, then it is rapid and probably has carved a gorge for itself. The meandering river lower down will flow through marshland unless this land is drained with small canals. In general, the river system governs the siting of towns and cities and road bridges – and hence bottlenecks – before engineers carved motorways through the landscape. (In the towns the bridges cause traffic jams, so try crossing the river before reaching the town if you have to continue on the other side.)

Gradients (see Diagram 7)

From contours to gradients; and this is a concept the motorist knows well. Gradients measure the steepness of the slope. At the roadside is a sign, 1 in 7, or 14% the equivalent – the percentage sign is universal through the Continent of Europe; 1 in 7 is the tangent of the angle in trigonometrical terms; that is, for each 7m travelled towards an objective, measured horizontally, one climbs – or descends – 1m. The gradient between two contour lines on a map can be measured. If the vertical interval between the contours is, say, 10m and the distance on the road 80m from one contour line to the next, then the gradient would 1 in 8.

Many road maps mark steeper sections by an arrow, pointing in the direction of ascent. A one arrow system may indicate a slope steeper than 1 in 7 or 14% as shown by the Ordnance Survey 1:250,000 in UK and by Kümmerley + Frey on the Continent of Europe. Michelin has its own one to three arrow system. One arrow 5 to 9%, two arrows from 9 to 13%, three arrows greater than 13%.

The Ordnance Survey has a two arrow system on larger scale maps – one arrow: 1 in 7, 14 to 20%; two arrows: 1 in 5 steeper, 20% and above.

As with conventional signs, study the information given before using that map. It is all there in the margins and base.

Finally, two ascending arrows facing each other indicate that there is a high point on the road in between and conversely, two arrows in opposite directions show that there is a low point in between. All this adds to the picture of the countryside. It also warns you if you are driving a heavy vehicle or towing a caravan. Military manuals lay down maximum gradients for various types of vehicles. Commonsense will tell you which road to avoid with a line of vehicles (see Conventional Signs Diagrams A and C).

Intervisibility

Gradients feature in problems of intervisibility and dead ground. Can one point be seen from another? Diagram 8 shows the

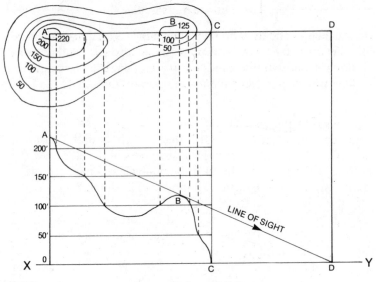

Diagram 8 Intervisibility

problems of an observer at point A on a hilly island (islands usually are hilly, otherwise the sea would flood them).

There are two questions:

(i) can the beach at point C be seen from the OP at A?
(ii) at what point would a boat approaching the island be seen or disappear from view?

The problem can be solved arithmetically; here is the diagrammatical solution.

There are four stages:

(i) draw base line, XY on **Diagram 8** on which to build a framework of heights of the same vertical interval as the map
(ii) project downwards from the map the points at which the line AC crosses the contour lines
(iii) make a cross section of the island and at once you know that beach C cannot be seen from point A
(iv) by projecting the line AB it is established that any boat nearer to the shore than at D could not be seen from A.

However, be wary of the converse, ie *what will definitely be seen?* It all depends. Intervisibility diagrams give negative answers, *what will not be seen*. Point B may be covered with trees so that a boat would not be seen much further out than D.

Note also another limiting factor – the curvature of the Earth.

This method can be used only for short distances, up to 5 to 10km. For at 20km an observer at 100m height A, wishing to see another observer at the same height 20km away, B would be obstructed by a midway point higher than 93m, C (see **Diagram 9**).

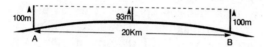

Diagram 9 Intervisibility and curvature of the Earth

The virtue of a diagrammatic method is that it can solve a number of problems at the same time; straightway the rôle of point B can be seen in obstructing the view from A. (Gradients will give a quick answer. The slope from A to B is less steep than from A to C and therefore B obstructs the line of sight from A to C. This answer turns on arithmetical accuracy.)

To summarise the procedure: in general, to solve an intervisibility problem diagrammatically:

1 Join the two points, as given in the problem by means of a pencil line.
2 Draw an equivalent line on a sheet of paper and set up a similar framework as in **Diagram 8.**
3 Mark on the edge of a sheet of paper the points at which the pencil line crosses the contour lines on the map.
4 Transfer these points on to the framework.
5 Draw the section from the data.

Section 5: Bearings: Direction

Approach

Bearings *measure* direction, as explained in Elements of Route Finding. The concept is so simple, that of giving direction in degrees or mils, instead of a hopeful wave of the arm, or left or right. Yet so many problems in map reading and navigation are concerned with bearings. Many become apprehensive, maybe because calculations are involved, especially when dealing with three Norths instead of one and there are back-bearings as well as forward bearings. When to add? When to subtract? The map user is also not helped by the current Ordnance Survey method of showing the three Norths in the margin of its maps. These lack a simple statement of magnetic variation from *true North* (see

Diagram 12). You really have to think when using the OS diagram.

There is no option but to master the subject, and that goes for the use of the new technology, too. The computer also deals in bearings.

Yet bearings need not be offputting. You need first to become quite clear about the concept, and then to use diagrammatic methods – a rough diagram will do – in tackling conversion of bearings, first just to record the information. You will note throughout this book my prediliction for diagrammatic methods. It is easy to present 'automatic' rules, *but* it is possible, especially under pressure, to become confused as soon as you ask, 'do I add or subtract?'. (One short cut, as used by the orienteers is shown at the end of this section.)

The difficulty with a purely arithmetical solution is that there is no check on whether the answer is correct or not – you can only hope. Moreover, data alters from year to year and place to place. The variation of magnetic North differs; that which has to be added in England may have to be subtracted on the USA West Coast. It is important to appreciate why you must solve the problems of conversion of bearings. On the map a grid bearing is measured with a protractor, but you **move** by the magnetic compass, so you must convert the bearing from the map.

First develop the concept of a bearing. Return to **Diagram 1**. The railway station is at 270° from point A, or 4,800 mils. What is meant by 270°? Imagine a line running to the North *through where you are standing*. Measure the angle turned in a clockwise direction, through which you had to travel from this North line to a line running to the railway station. This 'angle turned' would be 270° or 4,800 mils.

The bearing is measured:

(i) from a line running to the North through where you stand
(ii) always in a clockwise direction.

As you alter your position you alter the bearing. *On no account measure a bearing in an anti-clockwise direction*. Furthermore, a bearing is always calculated from a given position; if you do not know a position accurately you cannot plot the bearing from it. To overcome this use back-bearings, which will be discussed later.

Use of Bearings

Thus, bearings give direction. This is of value not only in following a route, but in locating a position. With ordinary bearings (forward bearings) it is possible to chart a position on a map which cannot be reached on the ground. For instance, you can see a point on a ridge in front of you. You could take a bearing on it from one point, and then take a second bearing from another point. When you have plotted the two bearings, you know that the point is at the intersection of the two bearings. Before you can do this, you need to know, firstly, how to take a bearing in the field, ie use of the compass; secondly, how to plot a bearing on the map, ie use of a protractor; thirdly, how to convert the bearing taken by a compass to the bearing plotted on a map.

Back-Bearings
In **Diagram 10**, you are at O. Imagine somebody at P. If this person at P took a bearing of you at O, what would that bearing be? From

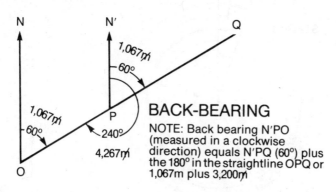

BACK-BEARING
NOTE: Back bearing N'PO (measured in a clockwise direction) equals N'PQ (60°) plus the 180° in the straightline OPQ or 1,067m plus 3,200m

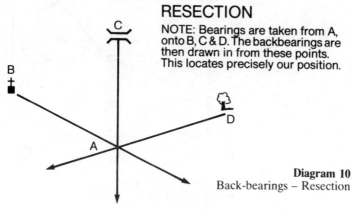

RESECTION
NOTE: Bearings are taken from A, onto B, C & D. The backbearings are then drawn in from these points. This locates precisely our position.

Diagram 10
Back-bearings – Resection

53

the diagram it can be seen that the bearing NOP is 60° (1,067m̃). The bearing NPO is equal to NPQ, plus the 180° (3,200m̃) contained in the straight line OPQ which equals altogether 240° (4,267m̃); 240° is the back-bearing of 60°; 60° is the back-bearing of 240°.

When calculating back-bearings.

(i) if the bearing is less than 180° or 3,200m̃ **add** 180° (3,200m̃)
(ii) if the bearing is greater than 180° (3,200m̃) **subtract** 180° (3,200m̃).

Certain protractors, as in the services, show forward and back-bearings on the same line.

Use back-bearings when you are in a position which you cannot

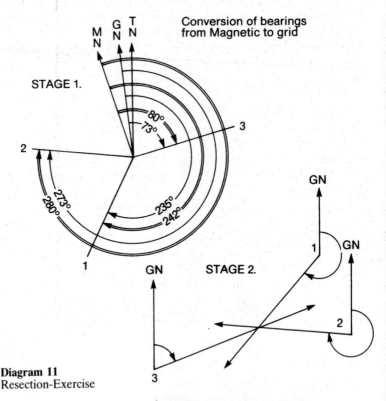

Diagram 11
Resection-Exercise

NOTE: Two bearings will fix a point. The third bearing serves as a check. This example, (taken from an actual situation in the field), is not ideal, it would have been better if the lines crossed each other at a sharper angle.

locate accurately on the map, but from which you can see other points *identifiable* on the map. Take bearings on these other points, and by adding (or subtracting, as the case may be) 180° to or from these bearings calculate back-bearings. Draw in these back-bearings; the forward bearings you took, you could not draw in since you were not sure of where you were. This process is known as **resection** (see **Diagrams 10 and 11**).

In the diagram you are at A and can see a church with a tower at B, a bridge over a stream at C and a windpump at D; B, C and D can be identified on the map. Take bearings on B, C and D. Calculate the back-bearings on these three points, trace them in on the map and their point of intersection will be your position. Before doing this however, *you must convert the bearing taken in the field to the bearings measured on a map.*

(In resection the main task will be that of choosing identifiable suitable points on which to take bearings. The rays from these points should cross at fairly acute angles).

Conversion of Bearings

You need to be clear on definitions; so to recapitulate:

A bearing measures direction. It is the angle between two lines that run through a point of origin. Line one points North. The second line points at the place on which you are taking bearing, in a clockwise direction.

There are three Norths. Firstly, there is North as given by lines of longitude, ie the direction of the North Pole or Pole Star (in the Northern Hemisphere) – **true North**.

Next, there is North measured by the compass, **magnetic North**, the direction in which magnetic North lies from any point in the world. This North varies from year to year and from place to place. It has nothing to do with a deposit of lodestone in Northern Canada – if it were, somebody is having a tough time moving it around from year to year!

Finally, there is North to which the grid lines point on the map – **grid North**. This differs from true North because a grid system superimposes a flat, squared network on the curved surface of the Earth. Therefore, grid lines are out of parallel with the lines of longitude. Grid North varies from map to map, and when handling a new map you should note at once the grid convergence.

The three Norths can be summarised as follows:

  (i) *true North* – the direction of the North Pole – measured by the lines of longitude – constant – (sun compass gives true North)
 (ii) *magnetic North* – the direction which the magnetized needle points to – measured by means of a prismatic compass – variation from true North differs according to time and place – the North people march or drive on
(iii) *grid North* – the direction of the grid lines – measured with a protractor – varies from map to map.

If you keep these three definitions in mind, then, whenever you take a bearing in the field you will know it is a magnetic bearing, or

STAGE I DRAW IN THE THREE NORTHS

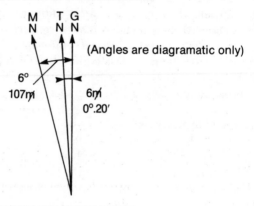

STAGE II DRAW IN YOUR BEARINGS

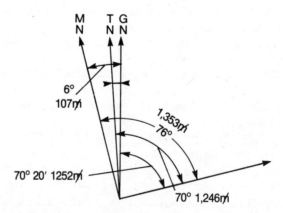

STAGE III BY INSPECTION READ THE ANSWER

Diagram 12 Conversion of Bearings by Easy Stages

if you measure a bearing on a map it is usually a grid bearing – if you consult an atlas it will probably be true North.

To show how to tackle a problem, imagine you have to go cross country from a road fork to the South East of Chipping Norton in Britain Ref NU 316.263. On the Oxford 1:50,000 OS map lay a protractor, its base parallel to the grid line running North and South, and you will find that the required bearings is 70°, 1246ṁ (see **Map A** on page 34). (How to use the protractor is described in more detail later).

Problem: on what *compass* bearing do you proceed? **Diagram 12** shows the stages.

   (i) at the side of the map is the information on the North points*. Note that the differences between grid North and other Norths . vary from one part of the map to another. If only one measurement is given, then it relates to the centre of the map. Here there are four measures. The one you need is that of the North West corner, near the start point.

     Now draw a diagram of the three Norths and fill in the figures. *Stage 1* From grid North to true North mark in 0°20′ (6ṁ). From grid North to magnetic North, the compass North, mark in 6° (107ṁ).

  (ii) *in stage 2* we draw the bearing of 70° (1,246ṁ) from grid North.

 (iii) *in stage 3* read the answers. The compass bearing is 76° (1,353ṁ).

The use of a diagram instantly solves the problem of whether to add or subtract. It is all there before you.

Of ⁺he three Norths the true North is the constant one; and you would be using it if you operated by the Pole Star at night. It is the North in lines of longitude.

As stated the other Norths vary from map to map and even from one part of the map to another. In the USA West Coast, magnetic North will be to the East of true North, the reverse in Europe and in the Middle East.**

---

*The difference between magnetic North and the other Norths decreases in this area from year to year and in three years will decrease by about ½°, 9ṁ. Before using a map in a later year bring the North figures up to date.

**In England magnetic North lies 6½° West approx of true North. True North coincides with grid North on a line through the Midlands.

    In North America, true and magnetic Norths coincide on a line from Churchill on Hudson Bay, West of Chicago and South through Panama City. In San Francisco the magnetic North line runs 16° East of true North, whilst in New York the variation is 12° West.

    In Britain magnetic variation decreases half a degree in 3 years. The variation remains constant in San Francisco and Chicago. New York has a westerly increase of 1° in 12 years (1986 figures).

Bearings (ii) The Compass
A compass gives us a bearing in the field. Two types are used mainly:

(i) the liquid magnetic (prismatic) hand compass, using a bearing measured by a protractor on a map (see **Photo 1**);
(ii) the lightweight compass as used in orienteering. It incorporates a protractor and, placed on a map, quickly gives the bearing (see **Photo 2**).

In this book in a later section I shall describe a sun compass for use in desert terrain. Cars, trucks and tanks may also be fitted with special magnetic and gyro compasses.

Later I shall describe the use of the lightweight compass.

When handling a prismatic compass

(i) keep the compass away from *all* metal
(ii) hold the compass firmly with the right thumb through the loop. With a liquid prismatic compass, the left hand will be free – but otherwise the left hand will be used as a front support, with the index finger on the check plunger
(iii) keep the compass horizontal
(iv) line up the hair line on the lid of the compass with the object. Then look through the prism onto the line and the card simultaneously
(v) as with a rifle, do not stay up too long in the aim; if the card is looked at too long the figures will fade out
(vi) if an accurate bearing is needed, take three bearings and see whether they agree.

For night work the liquid compass is most effective. It has a graduated outer ring. Any given bearing can be set by revolving this outer ring. The compass is used with the lid and body in one straight line. To march on a given bearing when the compass has been set, the compass should be manoeuvred round until the luminous diamond, or triangle, indicating magnetic North, is under the white dash on the glass of the compass. The luminous dashes at the two ends of the hairline on the lid of the compass give the direction of march. (Part 3 under 'Aids to Route Finding' discusses further the use of the compass, both by day and night.)

Protractor
(See **Diagram 5**). To lay off a bearing from a given point, draw or imagine a line through that point parallel to the grid lines running up the map.

As stated earlier, the protractor is laid to the *right*, if the bearing is less than 180° (3,200m); to the *left*, if the bearing is greater than 180°.

The little arrow in the centre of the base of the protractor should point to the place from which you are measuring your bearing.

To measure the bearing of one place on another:

(i) join the two places with a pencil line and extend the line in both directions

(ii) lay the protractor with the small arrow pointing to the point of intersection of the pencilled line and the nearest grid line to the place from which you are taking your bearing, laying the base of the protractor along the grid line.

Finally, on the reverse side of a Mark IV protractor is a useful set of scales with which to measure distances on Ordnance Survey maps.

Independent Compass Error

The modern liquid compass is reasonably accurate and less subject to the error which arose through the wear on the pivot of the old-time compass. Manuals discuss independent compass error and give rules on how to allow for it. There are procedures to establish deviation. However,

(i) conversion of bearings is a complicated process already and now there is an added factor

(ii) in the field are many other sources of error

(iii) moreover, often you will be handling a strange compass and will hardly have the opportunity to measure its error. *Only in surveying does the independent compass error become important.*

The Lightweight Compass (see Photo 2)

Before World War II, a Swede decided to shortcut the process of using a protractor on a map to read bearings and a compass by which to operate in the field, by combining the two in the **Silva Compass**, the Military version designated by the Ministry of Defence as : The Compass Magnetic Unmounted Lightweight (W10/6605995212576). This instrument has become the seeing eye of orienteers.

It has many advantages. It is light, easy to use and cheaper than the standard liquid magnetic. Bearings on the map can be read with it. It can be used in the open and carried easily by a cord.

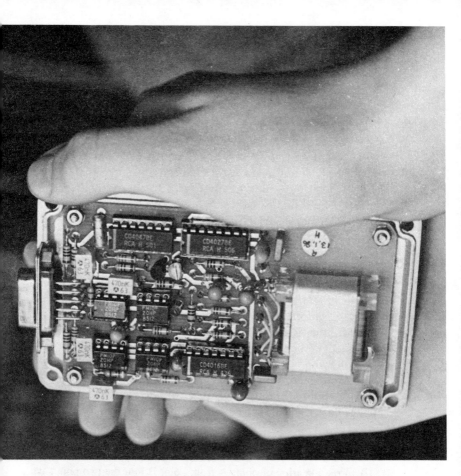

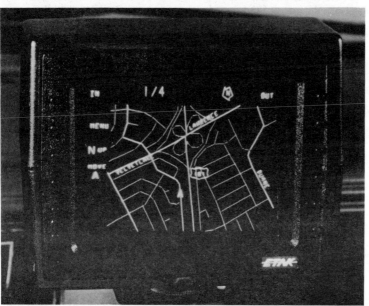

The standard version is calibrated in degrees. The military in mils, with degrees in smaller figures in the base.

The instrument includes rules in metric and imperial measures; a romer; a right angled measure to pinpoint reference points; a magnifying 'bubble' and a small luminous strip or patch.

However, for *accurate* recording and for night work, the lightweight compass has drawbacks. One cannot sight on an object in the open with the same precision as a standard liquid magnetic compass. True, one cannot march or drive on a precise bearing, within a degree or so or within 20 to 30m. As explained in the sections on Route Finding the compass is used mainly to sight landmarks on which to march or drive – and the landmark may be to one side or another of the bearing.

In a static position for surveying and where accuracy is essential, then the liquid magnetic is an advantage. As for night work, where a compass is most needed, a torch may have to be used in conjunction with the lightweight compass. Its luminous strip is not adequate. The liquid magnetic can be used on its own. There are conditions where a torch is not practicable.

The three main uses of the lightweight compass (Silva Compasses [London] Ltd at 76 Broad Street, Teddington, Middx, supplies easy-to-read instructional leaflets) are, briefly:

1 To read a bearing on a map

  (i) to read bearing of point A from point B join the two points with the edge of the outside protractor, pointing towards B
  (ii) turn compass needle housing to line up grid North on map with North on housing rim of compass
  (iii) read mils or degrees on pointer (forget the compass needle).

2 To travel on a bearing

  (i) before doing so convert the grid bearing from the map to the magnetic bearing. In the UK this will mean adding the magnetic variation, *but* as already stated, check it out on a rough sketch, at least for the first time. In California subtract magnetic variation but again, check out the variations, on a diagram.
  (ii) now turn the compass housing to line up your required bearing with the index point
  (iii) now move the whole compass horizontally until the magnetic North needle coincides with the magnetic North red arrow on the compass
  (iv) your compass is all set, for all you have to do is to follow the arrow at the end of the bubble.

3 To Take a Bearing in the Field

 (i) hold the compass horizontally and point it at the place on which you want to take a bearing
 (ii) turn the compass housing until the red arrow lies precisely under the red and white needle
 (iii) read the answer on the compass housing. If you have a compass in mils and degrees, then the degrees will be in small numbers at the base in very small figures, and not too easy to read I regret! In areas subject to strong magnetic dip the needle may foul the compass case.

Short Cuts

 (i) you need to take a bearing in the field – hence a magnetic bearing – and mark it on the map, a grid bearing. Now, instead of pointing the compass needle to North on the dial in step (ii) – on page 00 – point it to 354°, ie you have adjusted for the variation for grid North. This holds generally for Britain. In California you would adjust the other way. So you can read the grid North straight away. This practice can be followed when setting a map, the first stage of using a map in the open (Part 3). Some orienteers mark their compasses this way with a piece of tape.
 (ii) it is also possible to use a short cut when trying to locate one's position without the elaborate triangulation of bearings from different points, as described earlier. *That triangulation is needed for position.* If on a distinctive, long feature, a road or river and you want to know approximately where you are and can see a distinctive landmark nearly square on, then point the compass at the landmark and in England turn the dial to 354°, set the long edge of the compass on the map to touch the point you have sighted but then turn the whole compass until the orienting lines are parallel to grid lines. Your point on the road or river is, roughly, where the compass edge crosses it. Sounds complicated? It just needs practice.

As with all short cuts you must decide how accurate you need to be. The preceding sections spelled out textbook procedures. It is essential to do so in this book. However, if calculations can be circumvented by all means do so.

The principle of adjusting the compass beforehand can be applied to many situations.

Compass Traverse

Two sets of exercises teach the use of a compass; resection (see **Diagram 11**) and compass traverse.

In **Diagram 13** is an example of a compass traverse. The traverse in the example is not intended to serve as a rigid model but rather as a general guide.

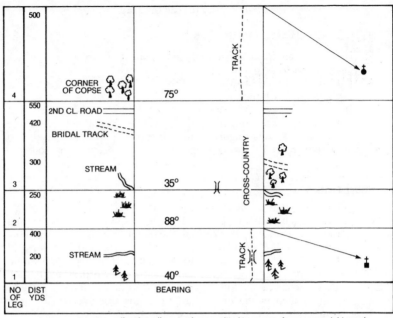

A compass-traverse on the above lines can be committed to memory for use on a night-march

Diagram 13 Compass-Traverse

The traverse in Diagram 8 was calculated from a map with a view to use on a night compass march. The bearings and principal distances were committed to memory,* and the route was followed without reference to a map. Such a practice would prove very useful in operations where one cannot afford to show a light – even a hooded torch – in consulting a map.

Traversing is usually associated with surveying, and the same principle of recording bearings applies for the purpose of route finding. In surveying, the traverse would consist of a series of legs with bearings to each side to define accurately the points in the area to be surveyed. On this basis a completed map is constructed from the traverse.

In compiling a traverse for a survey, both forward and back-bearings should be taken of each leg. For example, if Diagram 8 were part of a survey you would take a back-bearing at the end of the first leg as a check on your work, ie 120° to a church (2,133m) forward bearings become 300° (5,333m) back-bearings.

---

*400m on 40° compass bearing, followed by 250m on 88°, where a stream is crossed by a bridge, 450m on 35°, **(Diagram 8)** crossing a road at 400m and so on!

Part 3
Route Finding

Introduction

Part 1 outlined the elements of route finding, based on the three factors: reference points/landmarks, direction and distance.

Part 2 moved on to the reading of the map and the picture of country built from it, together with direction, bearings, compass and protractor.

Now to move outdoors with the map, and to apply the principles of route finding to a range of situations. This entails referring back to the first two parts of the book; where needed I will recapitulate and summarise briefly the points made in previous sections.

Part 3 begins with map setting. This is the first step when using a map in the open. **It must become a habit whenever you consult a map outdoors. It guards against moving in the wrong direction.**

Section 1: Map Setting

The First Stage in Handling a Map

Map setting means that when you open up a map you line up the features on the map with the corresponding features on the ground. Alternatively, setting the map means lining up North on the map with North on the ground. For instance, if there is a railway track running straight across the country ahead, it will occupy a corresponding place on the map. If there is a wood to the right on the ground, it will be to the right on the map, and so on. This principle of map setting is the first stage in handling a map in the field. Each time you consult your map line up the features on the map with features on the ground. It may mean that when moving towards the South, the map may be upside down, but, with practice, you will find that the advantages outweigh any difficulty in having to read names upside-down.

Map Setting by the Shadow Cast by the Sun

The easiest way of setting a map – even though the answer given is

65

Diagram 14 South by the Sun

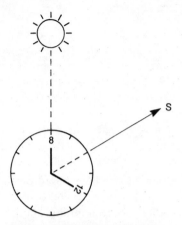

Point hour hand of watch at the sun
then halve the angle between the
hour hand and 12 on the watch face
– this points to south (for summer
time halve the angle between the
hour hand and 1)

only approximate – is to note the direction of the shadow cast by
the sun. Then by an elementary calculation, you can quickly
determine South, and so set out map (see **Diagram 14**).

Map Setting by Compass
A map can be set with a compass. At the side of the map will be
found an arrow pointing to magnetic North.* After bringing the
magnetic North up-to-date, all you have to do is to open your
compass out flat, lay the compass over the arrow on the map and
turn the map round until the direction of magnetic North on the
map coincides with the direction given by the compass.

Map Setting by Natural Features
You may not always have a compass; however, setting a map by
the natural features is a useful practice in all map reading, for by
so doing you can locate your position. **Diagram 15a** shows a sketch
of a map laid flat on the ground lined up with the features on the
landscape. The bridge over a stream on the ground is in the same
line as the bridge on the map. The line on the edge of the wood
corresponds to the edge of the wood on the map, and the church
with a tower is in line with the church on the map. The map is thus
set.

---

*Having brought magnetic North up to date see section on 'Conversion of Bearings' (Part 2).

It may not always be possible to pick out such features for the purpose of setting a map, but a little ingenuity will soon reveal certain features by means of which the map can be set. If a map is set roughly, the final setting follows; one identified feature, plus an estimate of the distance from that feature, will help to locate the position.

To locate position, use a straight edge along which to sight various landmarks and draw a line on a piece of tracing paper and so get the coincidence of two or more lines of sight, using tracing paper over the map. Even without tracing paper, the same principle can be applied with the use of a straight edge, although it may mean marking the map. A rough idea may be obtained quite easily without any markings at all.

In **Diagram 15b** a useful concept has been illustrated. When on a straight feature, such as a railway, road, or even a ridge of hills, it may be sufficient to get the bearing on just one feature which can

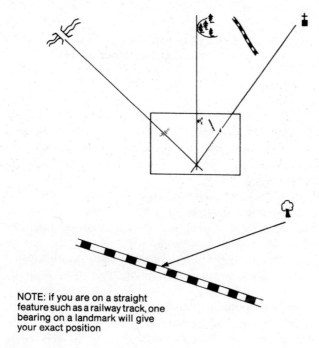

NOTE: if you are on a straight feature such as a railway track, one bearing on a landmark will give your exact position

Diagram 15a & 15b Map-setting by Natural Features & Locating Position

67

be identified accurately on the map, for the purpose of locating your position. Even without a compass this can be done quite easily, by lining the map up with the feature on which you are standing and then looking at the landmark on the ground and its corresponding representation on the map. This method can be applied in many ways, and is easy to use in action.

You know where you are
You are now ready to find your way
You must make sure you take the right route
But first here is a summary of what you should have done before you set out

1 You would have defined objectives and followed the drill as set out on the first page of Part 1.
2 Having planned the route you would have devised a system to memorise its main points.

Basically any system must:

   (i) be legible, easily read
  (ii) show main landmarks, identification and waypoints
 (iii) show direction
 (iv) indicate distances in time as well as in kilometres or miles
  (v) warn where you might go wrong – decision points
 (vi) in the case of the user being on wheels, especially, include antici-patory landmarks, to give an alert 3 to 5km in advance.

Obviously you cannot remember every detail but at least memorise the main landmarks, directions and distances. Work in bounds on foot or on wheels to the next point where you can stop and take stock.

You can help yourself by devising an elementary system to aid memory, a simple route diagram or a card with names or initial letters and simple signs, including one to warn where you might go wrong (see Part 4).

You have taken a decision. If you are uncertain you risk losing your way. Confidence is needed in route finding.

Keeping Direction/Directional Framework

Most problems of route finding resolve into a question of main-taining direction (see 'Direction Awareness' in later section). The measurement of direction was discussed in the sections on bear-ings. Now there is the task of keeping direction as planned. But first here is a simple system, the directional framework, to help memorise directions in an area. Then I shall deal with the use of the compass, by day and by night, and the use of the natural features.

The basic directional framework in open country is given by the river system and the hills.

Is it possible to memorise the main directions? In most sections of the countryside, you may then be able to find prominent features – a ridge of hills, a river or canal, railway track or main road – by which to fix both your directions and the position of places in the area in a quadrilateral or other figure. The directional framework aids the study and memory of an area of the country and if you are forced off your route, you know which way to turn as soon as you see any of the features of your directional framework. (For a directional framework based on highways, see **Diagram 18.**)

Urban Directions and the Paris Cab-driver System

The concept of a directional framework can also be used in towns, where it proves most helpful. People tend to relate places and roads to a framework of roads, whose directions they know. In most towns you can do this – use four roads in a quadrilateral and fix other places and roads in relation to this framework. The quadrilateral can become a navigational circuit.

One of the most effective researches into urban navigation was conducted by the French psychologist, Pailhous, on how Paris cab-drivers found their way. Pailhous found that over the years a driver confined himself to a relatively small number of roads, even though his passengers had a wide range of destinations. Obviously a great number of their journeys would be to and from the railway stations or air terminals or to the airports.

But there is plenty of Paris besides; no end of hotels and restaurants. Yet, in spite of having to cover an area of at least 200sq miles, in practice the Paris cab driver managed to find his way by a very limited number of routes *structured by a series of grids, related to basic points*. There would be a central grid and an outer grid – a box within a box and roads linking the two. Any place in Paris would be envisaged in relation to the system, so also giving a spatial view. (The wise driver in Paris no doubt should learn the cab network as then he would know the roads to *avoid*, especially which bridges – and bottlenecks!)

I shall return to this in Part 4 on mobile route finding.

But now to the methods of maintaining direction once you have decided on your route.

Maintaining Direction by the Compass, by day and by night

A compass gives direction. However, operating cross country with a compass can prove a slow and laborious business unless you can line up your compass bearing with a 'sight-mark' ahead of you.

By day – and by night if visibility allows – if you work on a bearing, say, of 120° or 2,133m̂, look for an identifiable point ahead – maybe a gap or an isolated tree – *a point which cannot be confused with another*.

Apparently featureless country – a desert – presents other problems dealt with later.

However, in selecting 'sight-marks' it would be no use trying to follow a line that led to the middle of a clump of trees. Not only is the middle a vague place, but especially at night, it will be found that a group of trees seems to alter its shape as it is approached.

Both by day, in difficult country without any features on which to line up a compass, and by night, when it is dark, it will be necessary to work with a guide. It is impossible to maintain direction on your own with eyes down upon the compass – no-one can walk in a straight line without a guide. The best way of operating is for you, as map reader, to hold the compass in your hand and have a guide standing in front. Ask the guide to look back over his shoulder and note the direction of the compass. Then the guide walks out a certain number of paces agreed on *beforehand*, according to visibility, and stops. Note how far the guide is over to the left or right; go to the guide, correct him, and set him off on his next bound. Note:

(i) compass bearer and guide never move at the same time – but alternately

(ii) in certain situations do not shout to the guide at the end of a bound, 'two paces to the right', or whatever the case may be. Make a note of the distance and go to the guide and move him (sound carries a long way at night).

In open country by day this process may be speeded up in the following fashion: besides having a map reader and a guide in front, there is a third person well to the rear who lines up the map reader and guide whilst both are on the move together. If this third person also has a compass, fairly steady progress can be maintained, and all parties can move together simultaneously.

This can be applied to movement in a desert (see Part 5) including even a line of vehicles, where the navigator is in the *second* vehicle.

A problem with a compass, especially at night, is that of by-passing obstacles en route. In **Diagram 16** is an example of a wood being an obstacle on the line of route at night. There may be dense undergrowth which not only makes progress difficult but makes the maintaining of direction accurately, virtually impossible. Instead of trying the difficult course, it may prove easier to stop at the edge of the wood, turn off at right angles and go a sufficient distance until clear of the wood and count the number of paces in that direction. Then proceed in your original direction, the distance B C in the diagram. Add on to this the distance covered on the line of route, and then back at right angles, the same number of paces taken away from the original routes, and so start afresh at point D. It does not need a knowledge of geometry to see that points A and D are in one straight line (see **Diagram 16**).

If there is a pond or river to cross, you must identify a point on the opposite bank in line with your compass and work round to this point and carry on with the route. If this is impossible do the same as in the case of the wood. Finally do not allow yourself to be diverted by the slope of the ground in undulating country. You just have to exercise more care, especially in choice of sighting marks.

Diagram 16 'By-passing' Objects on a Compass March

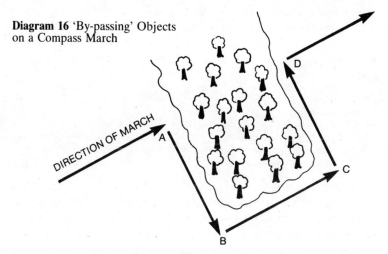

i) AB & CD are at right angles to line of march   ii) AB = CD

Maintaining direction by natural features and the elements
By day the sun is the best guide to direction. You know, from experience, the direction in which the sun shines at different times of the day. (Even if the sun is not shining, the sky seems to be lighter in certain parts, according to the position of the sun.) You can locate South with a watch as stated earlier (see **Diagram 14**).

At night the Pole Star in the Northern Hemisphere (see 'Night Navigation') gives true North, and the Southern Cross in the Southern Hemisphere gives us South – the other stars change their position, and if you see that the direction in which you have to travel points to a certain star, you must be careful to remember that the position of that star is constantly changing. Choose a star 30° up from the horizon preferably a degree or two less than the bearing on which you have to move – but only for 15 minutes then change it. If the night is very cloudy, a compass will be indispensable.

A prevailing wind helps to maintain direction, although its value is limited if you have to travel across country, sometimes sheltered by the trees and at other times by the undergrowth. However, if there is a strong wind blowing and you can feel the wind on your left cheek, then suddenly feel the wind on your right cheek, you may suspect you had doubled on your tracks.

Diagram 17 Locating North by the Pole Star

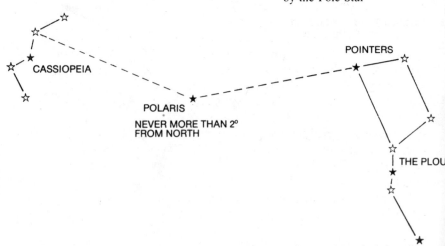

NOTE: In latitudes of the Middle East Cassiopeia is visible when the Plough is not.

At all stages remember the time factor. *It is very easy to forget the passage of time when engaged in a particularly engrossing task*; the sun that was in the South has moved to the West.

I have outlined the use of the stars, the natural elements and a compass in establishing direction, let me add,

(i) you cannot maintain direction with your eyes on a map, or on a compass; *you need to look ahead*

(ii) even if the sun is there in a clear sky as a guide, you must still seek a sighting point. In difficult terrain the sighting object will be nearer. Work in shorter bounds and be less ambitious.

(iii) in a tracked or wheeled vehicle with a built-in compass movement across country will still be from one sighting point to another.

(iv) so work from object to object. You cannot maintain a given direction if you keep your eyes on the ground immediately in front.

(Later, in the section on sun compass, it will be shown that where a shadow is cast that can be seen clearly as a guide, it is possible to operate in a general direction guided by the shadow of the needle. But ideally the sun compass is used with *sighting points*, if they can be identified.)

Section 2: Aids to Route Finding

Introduction

This section amplifies the principles already outlined. Some of the points come under fieldcraft, an adjunct to map reading and route finding.

First comes commonsense, sense of country – and an awareness of direction. From experience of instruction, I know that many people can become more aware. Once upon a time everyone may even have had a *sense* of direction, but the veneer of civilisation would have smothered it. Those who seem to have a natural sense of direction and country may have developed their flair from observant travel. Through this experience they learnt to associate one set of features with another; where a track will lead to or what is beyond a field. The flight of birds, even the movements of animals, are all guides.

How far man ever had – or some still have – an innate sense of direction is a subject I shall return to.

Commonsense

The first aid to all route finding, and the key to successful map reading is the use of commonsense. **Think!** No use applying this rule, or any other rule, in a mechanical fashion – **one must think**. One can cite examples of the use of commonsense in route finding and they usually arise when the map has to be bridged with reality. Commonsense can tell what the map maker through necessity has to omit from the map.

For instance, you are following a track through a wood, and in the middle of the wood the track forks. The fork, however, is not shown on the map. Both tracks are as wide as each other. Yet, because of the twisting nature of tracks in the wood, you cannot decide which track to take solely on the basis of direction (this problem is parallel to that of a motorist facing an unexpected divergence of roads.) One track however gives the appearance of not having been used recently. It probably leads to a woodcutter's shack that is rarely used – but the other track definitely gives the appearance of being in constant use. There are fresh ruts and according to the map the track should lead to a farm. It is obvious which track to take. This is a simple example but the principle holds good. On the other hand beware of following without question tyre marks. They can lead to a dead-end (see Part 5 on desert navigation).

Even sense of smell can find the right route. A wide river had been crossed in darkness by boat and the problem was to find a dry route across the marshes to a village. After walking a short distance down the bank in the probable direction we could smell hay. A haystack implied dry ground, farm buildings and obviously a dry route. Sure enough, in following the smell of the hay, a gate was reached which showed signs of being well kept and led to the farm buildings and the village.

Sense of Country and Layout of Towns
This book has accented what a map portrays, the country. The so-called 'sense of country' is but a natural result of the study of the country, in an intelligent fashion. Always observe. Map reading training is useless unless you do so. Through observation, you begin to associate certain features with each other. One type of grass means a river or stream at the bottom of a field and so on.

A parallel to this sense of country can be found in the statement, 'You couldn't lose me in a town. Wherever you drop me I'll find my way around'. This traveller has observed a *pattern* about the layout of towns – and even in a strange town he will find his way about from the experiences he has rationalised from other towns.

There is a distinctive layout of a city or town in Europe *governed by river crossings*, going back many centuries – and a different layout in many parts of the USA. A radial pattern, roads like spokes from a hub in European centres – and a grid pattern often in the USA.

Direction Awareness

I have dealt with maintaining direction at length, let me add here a more contentious matter – awareness of direction, the 'nose' some people *seem* to have for locating directions. Experience and observation are again the teachers. How best can one become more aware of direction? In Part 1 you are told to *think* direction. In which direction do you go from home to the office or station? You may find directions form part of a pattern. Observe; the road leading to the garage leads North because the sun sets in the West each evening on the lefthand side and you know that the same road leads South as you return home, for the North Pole Star is behind you on a clear night. You learn through your eyes (repeat **Exercise 5**). Practice is the teacher.

The Directional Framework

Let me illustrate further this concept outlined earlier.

However one travels, on foot, on wheels or tracks, this concept is used in studying – and memorising – the directions in an area of the countryside from the map.

Diagram 19 (page 90) shows a road directional framework whereby the position and direction of places West of Derby can be identified. It is based on a framework (see Section 7 for an example in the USA):

1 the Derby; Burton-on-Trent; Lichfield road A38 running South West.
2 Derby; Hatton; Uttoxeter road (A516 and A50) which is mainly West, though at first West South West, then slightly North of West.
3 the Ashbourne Road, A52, North West.
4 the North–South A515 from Ashbourne to Sudbury, then to Lichfield.

In the diagram is marked the village of Longford which can be related to the A52, A515 and to Derby. You can relate other places in the same way, and directions of roads.

75

Add to the directional framework by noting the natural features. Study a map and you will see that the River Dove flows West North West from the A38 to Uttoxeter, then turns North, with a tributary the River Churnel to the North West, whilst the Dove goes North East to Ashbourne and then North to Dove Dale. There is a low hill system to the North of it, before it turns at Uttoxeter and one can see the streams flowing into it. The river shows there are hills on both sides of the Uttoxeter–Ashbourne route and there into the Pennines, which dominate the North West of this area. The tributary Churnel cuts through to the canal to Leek. Follow the contours at wider intervals and you can see the shapes of the country emerging – and directions of the slopes.

Further Aids to Route Finding

A Useful Aid to Reaching a Position on a Road, Railway or any Straight Feature. The Principle of Deliberate Error

This section describes a useful aid in route finding. Orienteers call it 'aiming off'. It is a concept that was developed many years ago and was called the principle of deliberate error and it has its limitations. It should only be used if the point you are making for is located on a straight or *unique* feature. For instance, if the point is on a stream you must be sure that the stream has no tributaries to fool you. If on a road, then that no other roads join nearby which may well cause confusion. An edge of the marsh takes some definition. What is the edge? A railway is ideal and so is a stretch of coast or a wide river, a ridge or a distinctive road.

The principle is useful, of course, to the navigator of a boat at sea. But as with any method you need to use your wits in the application and make sure the circumstances are right.

Diagram 18 illustrates the principle of making for a place located on a straight feature. In **Diagram 18a** the problem is to go from point A, on a main road to a point B, on a railway line, where a bridle track meets the railway. The countryside is covered by woods and heath, intersected by tracks. The place to be reached on the railway cannot be seen until one is right on top of it. What do you do?

Instead of striking for point B, make for a point C, a kilometre to the north of B. By so doing you know that even if you miss point C by a few hundred metres, you would still have to turn due South

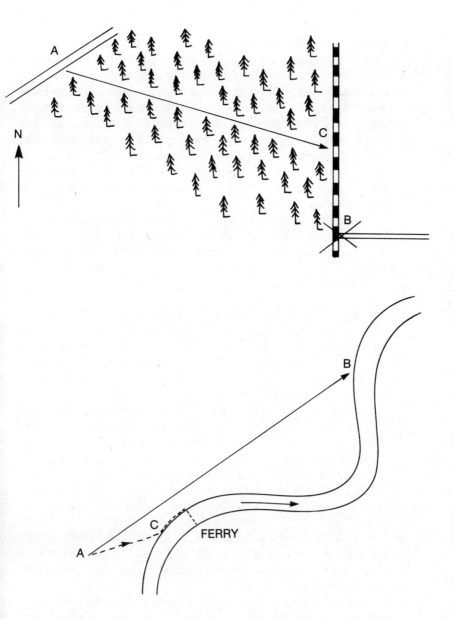

Diagram 18a & 18b A Useful Principle in making for a Place on a Road, Railway, River etc

as soon as you reach the railway line. (If you make directly for point B and miss this point you would not know which way to turn.) The distance of C from B would depend on your estimate of probable error in travelling across country.

In the second example **(Diagram 18b)**, a traveller is proceeding across low-lying country near the mouth of a river, trying to make for a ferry, a flat-bottomed boat moored close to the bank. The traveller misses his direction – mainly because of his attempt to find a dry route across the country – and finishes up at point B further up the river. Apart from forgetting to check the distance covered, he would fare far better to make for point C and work his way along the river bank.

Both these examples illustrate a principle which can be applied in so many different cases. Whether making for a village on a road, or for a point on a line of hills, or for a point in the desert or a ridge or in a wadi – the method of tackling these problems is the same. Go for the 'possible'.

Keeping a straight line in Difficult Country*

The last principle raises again the problem of keeping a straight line in difficult country. In operating without a map and a compass, it proves difficult to maintain a straight line in country which is either well-wooded, undulating or covered with difficult undergrowth, or, which lacks an identifying feature.

In open country, if there are no landmarks, look up at the sky. If the sun is not shining however, you must work from object to object, even if you have to create these objects for yourself, ie make for a certain spot on the ground 50m ahead. By constantly looking back at the direction from which you have come, you can line up these 'marks on the ground'. This may be your only guarantee against walking in circles (see 'Desert Navigation' Part 5).

In a wood, lining up the trees may prove a safer practice than following the tracks, if they are animal tracks. Explorers who blaze a trail through dense woods, often mark the trees as a precaution against walking in circles.

As far as possible try to move in straight lines. You can soon lose direction if tracks curve or if you try to work your way *around*

Note: this is an extension of the earlier section on keeping direction.

an area. This principle of moving in straight lines is illustrated further in Part 4.

Finally, use landmarks intelligently! There is no need to go *precisely* from one to another. Keep them in sight, as in **Diagram 18c**, where instead of a difficult cross-country route, the longer but easier to follow route, ABCDE is taken. As said before, navigation is the art of the possible.

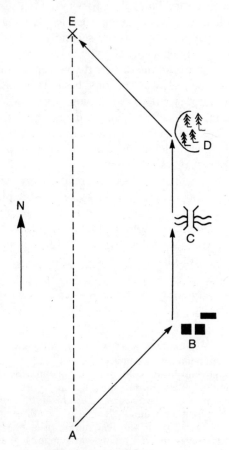

NOTE: Instead of trying to follow a difficult cross country route from A to E, fix the route by landmarks, B, C & D.

Diagram 18c Following a Route

79

Section 3: What to Do When Lost

First define the problem. What is meant by being lost? Is it just the feeling that something has gone wrong? Is this the right road or track? No this is not the right road and there is no indication where it leads. What is on the ground doesn't relate to the details on the map. Something went wrong on the way.

The problem is exacerbated in two ways. Firstly, the fear of being lost can lead to bad decisions, such as plunging on regardless, which in a way avoids decision; secondly, you may be navigating for others. Driving a car, everyone may have passengers all of whom *know* better than the driver. If you were leading a reconnaisance you may be too aware of some behind you just waiting to prove you don't know what you are doing. Forget whether or not you are losing face. The first thing to do is **stop**, at the earliest sensible point. You have less chance to think clearly if you keep on at all costs. Even with electronics you still must stop to get your position and consult the VDU.

On foot, this is less of a problem. There are many reasons to call a halt. In a car, then it is the next layby or parking place.

You may *hope* that you can drive on and work out what has gone wrong and somehow rejoin the planned route, but in minutes you may be ten or more kilometres even further on the wrong road. So here is the drill:

(i) **stop; rest; brew up tea or coffee** By stopping, not only can you consult the map, but you can think more clearly and plan ahead what to do. Do not go blundering on in the vain hope of rejoining the route. At rest the problem can be sorted out. Here the new technology comes into its own for it will locate a position. But most route finders need a procedure to follow.

(ii) **take stock of your position** On foot you can make for a higher point from which to survey the surrounding country. But to take stock, first **set the map**. See if you can line up the North line on the map with the North on the ground. Can the area on the map in which to look be narrowed? Can any landmarks, prominent features be identified and lined up with points on the map? Is there a road on the map in the direction of the road you have been travelling on?

(iii) **cast your mind back to the last point where you knew you were correct** Can you remember the route you took since the last correct point and see if you can trace this route on the map? How far have you travelled from that point? Can you swing an arc on the map? It may prove easier to trace the route back on the ground, ie go back to this last point where you knew you were correct. In doing this you may very often see where you went wrong, well before you returned to that last point.

(iv) **make a decision and stick to it** Decision can restore confidence – vital in route finding.

You may decide to go back, which is not an admission of defeat but is often wiser than trying to strike across country or traverse strange roads in the hope that somehow you may rejoin the correct route. In tracked vehicles across country or on foot decide on a compass bearing that will lead to a road or the coast or other feature, from where to turn towards your destination. Whatever your decision, carry it out boldly – and always aim to *travel in straight lines* rather than work round in an arc or part of a circle, whereby you will lose direction altogether. The simplest decision on wheels may be to continue to the next signposted road and then **stop** and appraise or go slowly back until you see a recognisable point. True, turning back runs contrary to human nature but most problems relating to being lost arise from failure to stop and think. (In a section on finding your way in special situations like no-name roads round an airport or industrial estate, I shall propose another step that many are reluctant to do. I shall tell the reader not only to slow down but if need be get out of the car to survey the scene and make a quick reconnaissance.)

This section on being lost also deals with fog, where one can easily miss a turning. Many just follow the tail lights of the vehicle in front but the truck ahead may be turning into a quieter road for a rest. In fog, more than at any other time, good planning before-hand is essential. Note the salient points, work out distances from one to the other and use the mileometer in the car, becoming alert 3 or 4km (or 2 miles or more) before making that turn. *Fog, of course, impairs one's judgement of distance and time.* People tend to believe they have gone further than they have on the ground when in fog. This is caused by more than having had to reduce speed.

Generally fog settles more on motorways or freeways than on the byroads and the older main roads. For the new roads enjoy cuttings into which the fog can drift and stay and they do not have the benefit of buildings close by to break the fog and raise the temperature of the road surface. Old roads, too, have landmarks and places to stop at. If the readers suspect prejudice, I plead guilty, but then a map will help one to find an alternative and quieter route.

So far route finding has been by means of a map. Here is an example *without* a map, for it shows how to apply principles of route finding and above all how to use commonsense.

Without a Map
Imagine a convict escaping from a penal settlement in the centre of an island covered with dense jungle. He escapes a few hours before dawn and he hopes to be able to reach the coast to pick up a boat waiting for him in a creek on the North coast; **the night is cloudy and there are no stars to guide him.** Furthermore, his position is complicated by the fact that in the scramble of getting away, he is not quite sure of the point of the settlement's perimeter from which he escaped. (*As an exercise, work out what to do before reading on.*)

Set down what he knows. Firstly, that the coastline is at a lower level than the penal settlement. Secondly, that any downhill direction he takes in a straight line will hit the coast or a stream that will join a river to the sea. What does he do? He keeps a straight line, until either he hits the coast or he reaches a river or stream to follow down to the coast, and so work his way round to the creek. Naturally, keeping a straight line in the darkness, through jungle, is difficult, and he may have to hack his way through the undergrowth, but if he constantly *checks the direction from which he has come*, it will help him to maintain a straight line. (The problem is being considered purely as a navigational exercise and not one of eluding his captors.) As dawn breaks he will know East and hence North, as his final guide.

The general principle is to make full use of knowledge of fieldcraft and country to assess what is to be done to maintain a straight line once it is decided in which direction to go, until reaching some identifiable object.

Anyone else, not the escaping convict, could make for higher country and survey the countryside in the hope of being able to locate his position.

Remember that the same principles apply when you are lost without a map, as with a map. Stop, take stock of your position, cast your mind back to the last point where you knew you were correct, make up your mind what to do and stick to it. The decision may be to carry on until you reach a place or area you know.

Psychological Note on Being Lost

One aspect of the drill on what to do when lost and retracing the route, would seem confirmed by the research of R. W. Byrne, Department of Psychology, University of St Andrews, on 'Memory for Urban Geography'. (*Quarterly Journal of Experimental Psychology 31*, 1979).

Byrne found that the subjects of his research assembled their information on the places in an area in a diagrammatic network, like the London Tube map, and not in a vector map, that shows distances and directions. Locations were seen like nodes on a string and it was sufficient to learn the sequence of locations for navigation, like a traveller on the Underground knowing that Green Park comes after Piccadilly Circus, if going West and then Hyde Park Corner and so on – or knowing the sequence of street numbers on the New York Subway. The distances do not matter nor the precise direction, for one has only to follow the sequence to get to the right station. Now if another route intersects, then it is like another string attached to the first, and there will be further strings. *But everything turns on sequence.* Road junctions – nodes – tie the strings to each other. As it does not become essential to learn distances and direction accurately, the traveller does not acquire a vector spatial awareness. So short cuts from a node on one string to that on another present a problem, *unless one retraces the route to the junction between them.*

The drill of what to do when lost advised you to mentally retrace to the last point, maybe physically, too. You knew you were right to that node on the string – and hence a warning against blind cross country attempts to rejoin your route, *because unless you know the area well you can get more wrong.* However, if you know the country well enough to cut across or to work you way through a maze of roads, you would not be lost anyway.

So to the vital point. The standard practice of route learning and following, the *network scheme*, leads to tunnel vision. To be proficient in navigation it is necessary to build up a picture of an area of country from the map so as to recognise the country beyond the road or track you are following. If you knew the area on either side then you would navigate better and that applies, too, to the freeway and to motorways anywhere.

If you have a spatial image instead of a string network, you can recognise landmarks well outside the road you are following. For the modern motorway too often lacks features and landmarks; it is an enclosed world.

Part 4
Mobile Navigation

To appreciate Part 4 – firstly try Exercise 8 – and repeat it – not only for the occasional journey – but for a regular journey in business or weekend.

(Part 8 deals with electronic navigation aids. Part 4 outlines the principles of navigation and map usage on wheels or tracks across country that apply *with* or *without* the new electronic technology.)

Background

Look inside a car – in the glove compartment – and there you'll find a map, maybe two or more. Now look on the highway and that car is stopped in a traffic jam or, notwithstanding road signs, takes a wrong turn or passes the right one. The story goes of a visiting pop star who could not get off the freeway in Los Angeles and finished up in Las Vegas, when all he wanted was the Hollywood Bowl and Universal Studios. Exaggerated? A similar scenario could be written, in many places in many countries – and the problems of mobile navigation do not end on the main highways. They multiply on poorly signposted minor roads, urban areas and in open terrain.

Why? There are maps; highways are numbered; there are road signs and drivers have eyes. So what is the problem?

The elements of navigation remain the same – routes are planned and followed, not by counting turnings but by:

(i) identification points and landmarks
(ii) direction
(iii) distance

Now, however, the scenario has been speeded up. The route finder moves ten to twenty times faster. Yet the same brain has to cope – observe, think decide, then instruct – when for each second of thought the vehicle has travelled another 73ft (22m) at a steady 50mph (80kph) and may be already past the turning.

Memory and the ability to recognise locations and road details

84

becomes most important. Hence the need for a *systematic* method to master and record route essentials and to be able to recall them on the way. Decisions must be taken well in advance. It is impractical to consult a map whilst driving.

So, *dictum one*: the key to finding one's way on wheels! **Plan first – then drive.** (The same principle applies of course for all navigation.) Ten minutes or more of study before setting out can save many times ten minutes on the road and save fuel and frustration. The trouble is that people are in a hurry – even before getting into the car. They may be unwilling, too, to take the trouble or indifferent map readers.

Now *dictum two*: **anticipate.** Sound navigation is anticipation, just as is good driving. So any plan includes an added element, essential in wheeled and tracked navigation – *anticipatory landmarks* as means of alerting the driver for action ahead. Study of the map shows an isolated bridge that will indicate 5km ahead – three minutes – there is a turn West on to a byroad, labelled (it is to be hoped) 'Church Heights'. That anticipatory landmark is essential to avoid depending on waiting until one reaches the sign to that turn. For from the vehicle – and from where one is in the traffic – one may not really see the sign and, worse, when it does appear its message may need working out. For instance, although the turn is the correct one, the sign may not read 'Church Heights' but may refer to somewhere else on that road – and then one must think fast.

Signs and their recognition are subjects in themselves. I shall return to this later. The approach, though, is that your plan must not depend solely on signs. In many urban and rural areas signs can confuse, as can their multiplicity and siting on the main highways. Hence a programme is needed to warn of what to do before reaching the signs; then when they are seen, their information proves a bonus.

So to the precept: **study first; plan.** How to do so forms the subject of the sections that follow. I shall explain in detail, examining each issue in a logical fashion – a necessary procedure in an activity too often dominated by compulsions – to hurry, not let anyone pass and to press on regardless.

But before I analyse the problems and work out the system to plan and follow, let me add *dictum three*: the **key to highway navigation**, especially of motorways and freeways, is to *know the territory on both sides*, know the shape and layout of the country, the urban patterns, know places and where roads lead to. Then you will rarely go wrong and will have flexibility to take another route if the motorway snarls to a halt.

Section 1: The Plan

Objectives and Purpose

The obvious: the purpose and urgency, if any, of a journey should determine the route, plus of course the physical factors – the vehicle being driven and the road systems used. For a cross country vehicle this includes the terrain. Now go through a check list:

(i) on business or pleasure? An appointment to keep? Plane to catch? Would half hour or more make all the difference? Do you want to avoid heavy traffic?

(ii) any places of special interest to see en route or the scenery?

(iii) does the vehicle restrict your use in any way, eg towing a caravan? Can it operate cross country or on very rough roads and tracks?

(iv) by day or by night and the weather?

(v) on your own or with other people and/or vehicles?

(vi) if military, security and cover?

The map enables you to be flexible. It gives you the options – the motorway – or a quiet route. The latter may even be faster; it depends – you cannot assume that the six-lane motorway means a clear route all the way.

Significantly, the Automobile Association in Britain advises members going on holiday to travel earlier on a Friday and also to drive through the night. This book isn't needed to remind you that on a late Friday afternoon the motorway can be solid in California, around Paris, around London or the Midlands.

Information

(i) there are no end of maps and guides available, some more suitable than others. These will be described, assessed and recommended in later sections.

(ii) road systems are labelled and numbered. It pays to learn the basic systems and classifications. In Britain roads with a 1 prefix go North and East of London; 2, South and East; 3, South West, etc. In the USA odd numbers on the Interstate highways go North and South and the even numbers, East to West.

(iii) there are road signs – in some countries clearer than others, especially in Continental Europe as compared to Britain – though Britain now has a Primary Route System which I shall describe.

Signs, which very much use numbers are fine on the main highways in the USA, but are not so good when you leave that highway.

(iv) your vehicle contains the most neglected navigational aid – the mileometer. **Landmarks plus distance pinpoint the turn you want and will anticipate that turn.** Hence, make sure the mileometer is accurate and visible and if need be install one with a trip counter easily seen without distraction by day and by night.

Maybe journeys could be planned by route numbers and place names. Many are, yet things still go awry. Moreover, such planning lacks flexibility. What can be done if, as in the Introduction, a hold-up stretches miles ahead or some factor obliges you to change your route? Problems divide into three groups:

(a) *environmental*: the nature and layout of the highway systems, motorways that disorientate and isolate the driver from the outside world. The identification of points in urban complexes aside from the poor signposting in rural areas.

(b) *physical*: the vehicle, problems of driving, traffic, visibility including seeing signs and landmarks from where the driver is.

(c) *psychological*: the ability to cope, one's memory which plays a greater part in mobile navigation than on foot, and the ability to recognise and identify places and routes from information gathered from the map. The need to decide, isolated in a vehicle, covering a distance whilst working out what to do. Clearly a map cannot be read on the move. That concept is a contradiction in itself.

A navigator may sit next to the driver but directing a driver is the art of the few – a subject I shall return to.

What then if you have to rely on signs? The clearest signs can still confuse. The exit for the motorway may be labelled Derby *South* or Frankfurt *Nord West*. You know that you want a 'Derby' or a 'Frankfurt' sign but are you sure that these are the right ones? For now comes that nagging element of doubt. How does one cope with a '⅔ Mile to Interstate 5' in California? Or, as the freeway often cuts across an urban conglomeration, the sign may only announce a street name or number. Is this it or isn't it?

Now for a physical problem; one's range of vision is limited. On foot it is possible to look around. On a cycle that is still possible, though limited. A vehicle restricts the range of vision and if the vehicle is military and on tracks, even more so.

Yet most people do find their way and do not get lost. On the other hand, in the belief they are taking the easiest and quickest option, too often they make for the same stretch of highway at the same time, when intelligent study and planning could reveal a

quieter and often a quicker route. **Try using the map to advantage.**
It pays to experiment – hence the exercises at the end of this book.

Solving the Problem: Planning Considerations

(i) any system is constrained by the nature of highways systems, motorways with limited access and exits.

(ii) no system should rely on a passenger sitting by the driver unless than person really knows his job. A rally team uses a navigator – but he is an expert, not only in route following but also in driving, in clarity of communication and in establishing a rapport. In the military world there would be some one directing. However, for most drivers this task cannot be delegated to a front seat passenger. The best use of a passenger is to equip him/her with a route checklist, and a memory prompt *which you have compiled –* described later. Naturally the passenger can hold the maps but a vehicle at speed in traffic is no place for a conference on which way to go.

(iii) one enemy of navigation and good driving is tunnel vision that limits the world to the ribbon of road ahead. *It is necessary to know beyond the highway.* Signs at the side can take one unaware. The extreme example is the night truck-driver who may know little beyond the tunnel created by the headlights and the stop-off place on the way. The same route could look strange by day. Finally, the fact that one has taken the outward journey does not mean it will be familiar for the return. This is soon learnt on foot. It applies equally in a vehicle, sometimes even more so. At least on foot one can turn around and note the view and features to identify the return route. That can hardly be done in a vehicle. *Hence, note identification points and landmarks on your journey which will help fix the route on the way back*, eg a turn opposite the Lion Hotel. Landmarks plus distance for your return route is a task to give to your front seat passenger – tell him to write down the points *as you note them.*

Section 2: Planning the Maps

In general in Britain and on the Continent of Europe at least two sets of maps are needed. In the USA three or more may be needed but the principle remains the same. *Begin* with a small scale map covering a large area for the overall plan and then *proceed* to a larger scale, more detailed map covering a smaller area and, if need be, urban and town maps (for maps in the USA see Part 7).

(i) *a small scale planning map*
In Great Britain, the Ordnance Survey 1:625,000, formerly ten

inches to the mile, is ideal. On the Continent of Europe the Michelin or the Swiss Kümmerley + Frey 1:1 million. Kümmerley + Fray publish a 1:2,750,000 for Europe from Lisbon in the West to East of Moscow. Michelin, whose motoring maps are a byword of clarity and good value, is extending its regional coverage from France and Italy to Germany and Scandinavia. In Italy, note the maps of the Touring Club Italiano.

AA Travel covers Europe in 1 to 1 million sectors, such as Benelux and Germany on one map. Germany offers a wide choice; the Länder, the states into which West Germany is divided produce their own series of maps (see later). Note schematic maps, especially the Ordnance Survey and motoring organisations that give a key to routes and distances in diagrammatic form – most useful in planning and a good concept to follow.

(ii) secondly, get hold of a *larger scale map* with more detail for the area to be visited, of the order of 1 to 200,000.

All the major map makers produce such maps in Europe (see later, 'Continental Motoring'). In the UK there is the option of single sheet maps, eg the OS Routemaster 1:250,000 series, each of which covers a wide area, such as from Dover in the South East to Birmingham in the North West on one map, or a bargain buy, the Ordnance Survey Atlas comprising 3 miles to 1in in England and Wales and 7 miles to 1in in Scotland, in one book. Bartholomew publishes all of Britain at 3 miles to 1in, for £1.70 more. The motoring organisations and publishers cover Britain in book form whilst the RAC has produced a series of Navigator Atlases to cover most of England and Wales in four books.*

These navigation atlases are 1 to 100,000, 1.6 miles to 1in and very clear indeed and a great deal of useful information on towns and places besides. Yet with the benefit of so large a scale they still omit contours, which the Ordnance Survey includes.

Bartholomew traditionally produced the 1:100,000 (formerly ½in to 1 mile) series for cyclists. The maps are clear. As motorway developments do not affect cyclists as they do motorists, then maybe it is not too important that two of the series I bought for different parts of the country were five and six years old.

Note: RAC motoring maps include:
  (i) Great Britain Atlas 4 miles to 1in
  (ii) Great Britain 10 miles to 1in Super Planner
  (iii) national maps for England and Wales (10 miles to 1in), Scotland and Ireland (both 8 miles to 1in)
  (iv) regional maps 3 miles to the inch.

Diagram 19
Directional Framework

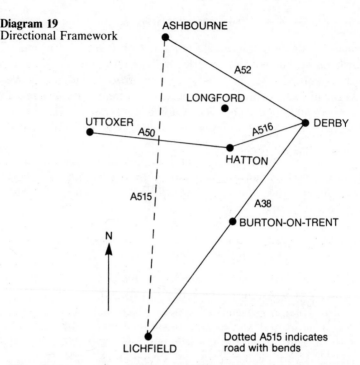

Dotted A515 indicates
road with bends

The Ordnance Survey also publishes Tourist Maps for such areas as Snowdonia in Wales, ½in to 1 mile. To study an area in detail it pays to have an even larger scale map, 1:50,000. Then it really is possible to plan alternative routes.

How to Study the Map: Revision for Wheeled Navigators
Titles are not enough. First make sure you know all about the map, its scale, the area and distance covered and any extra information it gives, eg camping sites, viewpoints – *and, above all, the date of the last revision and details of what has been revised.* Some commercial maps are very short on this necessary information. Today's maps can soon be dated. Road construction is continuous – and other features change.

Studying the map means more than looking for a few main highways. Apply the sequence from Part 2 to wheeled navigation.

(i) look for the natural features as on foot. If a road map does not include the river system, then find another map. Rivers give the first indicator of a shape of the country and also determine the siting of towns and hence the original road system. Modern engineers can excavate and carry highways over a viaduct or through a tunnel but even they have to take account of geography.

90

Rivers may indicate bottle necks on road bridges, especially in towns.

(ii) establish a directional framework so that you have a framework of the main natural features as well as of the highways. For any area there will be three or four, which could form a box **(Diagram 19)** and so places and roads can be related to this box.

This study of country, above all, helps to locate landmarks by which to fix and memorise routes (see later section on 'Suitable Landmarks'). The signs each side of the road will now mean something. Place names and shape of the landscape become recognisable. A line of hills appears to the West of the highway – as in the map. It confirms the route.

Map Road Information

A motorist's map will distinguish between:

(i) the motorways, freeways, roads with limited access and inter-changes

(ii) main highways, trunk roads and through roads, based on the older road system and whether they have been brought up to motorway standards, and with dual carriageways clearly shown

(iii) according to scale of map, minor or local roads (see **Diagram A** OS Conventional Signs).

In Britain the 'Primary Route System' of selected points and places throughout the country is shown in white letters on a green background on road signs and also is shown against a green background on up-to-date road maps. The system, non-motorway, is designed to get the driver from one place to another across the country in a sequence of places of major traffic importance. Not to be confused with French green and white system showing quieter roads away from the Autoroute.

Urban areas demand individual maps in that, particularly in the United States where gridworks of roads are close to each other on the map with names that need to be read, without a larger scale map those names cannot possibly be shown clearly. This especially applies in urban areas, where one needs a magnifying glass to distinguish one road from another. Good urban maps are treasures and it pays to compare one with another.

In general a larger scale map will show:

(i) road widths, where one may be held up behind a slow moving vehicle, fenced and unfenced roads

(ii) minor roads with a series of bends – near an estuary probably a marshy area; in the hills, if acute, indicating steep climbs, maybe a drop on one side – this information reinforced by arrows on the map indicating gradient greater than 14%, 1 in 7 or steeper (see Part 2), passing may be difficult, but the views usually are superb; not for heavy vehicles.

Some European maps and more so in Britain, mark strips of road with scenic views and show viewpoints off the road. Incidentally, unfenced roads do not necessarily enable a driver to get off a highway. The land may be farmed.

For the military, the nature of woods either side – conifer or non-conifer – indicate possible cover.

Larger scale maps help in the problem area – what happens when you leave the main highway system and have 15 to 30km or more – 10 or 20 miles – of byroads to your destination, on rural or urban areas where every road and street looks the same? This is where you can get lost. In this situation you really have to look for landmarks, reference points and, above all, to *identify them for sure by distance from one point to another*.

Finally, in studying the map, plan to judge distances on the map with the eye, especially as you will be switching from one scale of a map to another. So on a different map note the scale before studying it. Learn also to judge time on the map as well as distance (see Part 1).

You have studied the right maps. You have worked out the route but to make sure that you follow what you have seen on the map you need a route following system. In any system observation and memory play the key roles. So to the plan itself.

Section 3: Plan by Numbers – The Highway System

The simplest plan is to get onto the motorway system and off it at the other end nearest to your destination. It may involve interchanges but is easy to learn. For example, London to Blackpool, Lancs: M1, 78 miles to M6 (distance from start of motorway system), then 143 miles on M6 to M55 and 12 miles into Blackpool. The plan here is in miles since they are the distances shown on the road signs.

Or in the United States, from Columbus, Ohio to Memphis, Tennessee: Interstate 71, 169 miles to Louisville and Interstate 65 then 165 miles to Nashville and by Interstate 40, 158 miles to Tennessee.

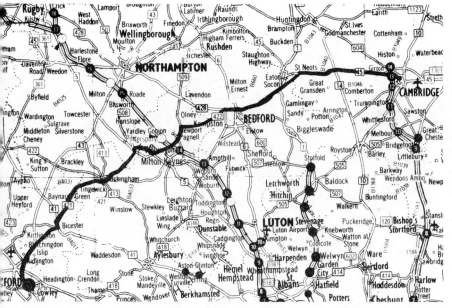

Map 1 RAC Recommended Route – Cambridge-Oxford (1″ equals 13½ miles, reduced)

One does not have to be a top rank map reader to plan this way. In Britain you could also use the Primary Route System, described earlier. The Royal Automobile Club in Britain, at least one part of it, is so impressed* by this system that when requested for a route from Oxford to Cambridge the official just sent a map with the route so marked, claiming one has only to follow the Primary Route System. (How other motoring organisations advise I shall come to later.) As regards the route from Oxford to Cambridge there are a few places where a stranger could go astray, as at St Neots and at Milton Keynes. A study of the map especially on a large scale will indicate such places where the driver has to look for the road signs, which in the UK are still not good enough. It pays to list them beforehand. More than a marked map is needed. Moreover, a marked strip along a road route on the map fosters the belief, described earlier as the chinagraph illusion, that the distinctive looking route on the map is a similar distinctive route

---

Note: interestingly, in contrast A. J. A. Lee also of the RAC in his paper to the NAV 85 Conference in York, was not so impressed by signposting in Britain. 'Difficulties are caused by deficiencies in the signposting systems and failure to maintain the signs satisfactorily so that they are legible.' Very much my experience which underlines the methodology of Part 4. A marked map depends too much on the clarity of road signs.

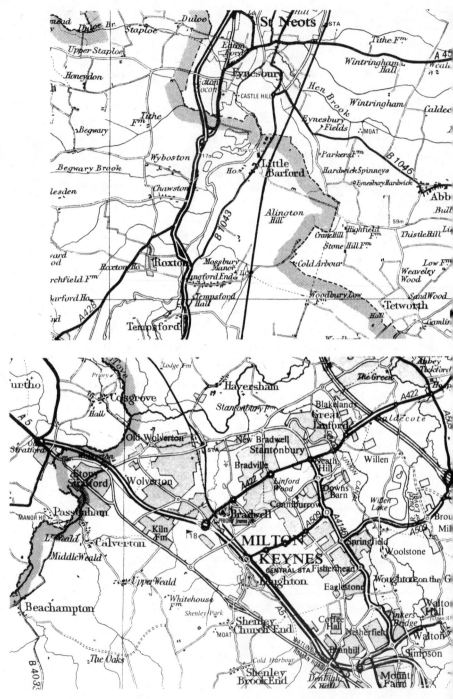

Map 2 Details from Cambridge-Oxford RAC Route, St Neots & Milton Keynes on larger scale map (Bartholomew, 1:100,000, enlarged)

on the ground. It is all laid out and there is little need for further thought – maybe?

The Motorway: Exit by Numbers

Whilst on numbers consider the motorway and the common problem of leaving at the right exit. Another section deals with the problem as an exercise in distance from a known reference point/ landmark – standard procedure in navigation. Furthermore, the key to motorway navigation lies in knowing *beyond the motorway* – the country and the roads. Now for standard practice, as used by many – simplicity itself. *Exit by numbers*! The map says Exit 7. So at Exit 6 get ready and look ahead. It is easy and commonsense. Of course, as with all good ideas, there are snags. Firstly, it depends on the direction of travel. It may be *Exit 8* that alerts you to Exit 7. You need to be sure. Secondly, it helps to know the distance from one exit to another, so that you can anticipate it well ahead to get into the right lane.

There is also the obvious question: *are the numbers always clearly marked on the road signs*? The signs carry other numbers of highways and distances, and numbers can confuse. Yet this does prove a sound practice to give advance warning, especially over a route you are going to use often.

So much for numbers! One needs systems to make sure, not depending on numbers or signs.

Landmarks and Distance

Now for the landmarks by which to structure the route and help ensure that you follow it. Landmarks by definition must be:

(i) unique in relation to surroundings
(ii) recognisable and most visible from a moving vehicle according to time of day

Landmarks are especially needed:

(a) to locate a turn or alert a driver to where he can go wrong
(b) above all to *anticipate* a turn or important point en route on any road or highway. Anticipatory landmarks are needed to ensure drivers leave the motorway at the right exit.

Is it possible to identify from the map some feature recognisable well in advance say, 5 or 10km, 2 to 5 miles? Now, both landmarks and more so, anticipatory landmarks, need not necessarily be on the highway. The end of a line of hills to the East of a highway can serve as a warning, or a river, *though it is important be wary in planning as to what may be seen from a highway*. As in the section on intervisibility (Part 2) you can be more sure of *what* you will *not* see than of what you will. A line of trees or a long fence at the side of the road can obscure the view. So seek most identification points on or near the highway – prominent features nearby will also act as guides. These include rivers, railroads, railway stations, bridges, viaducts, tunnels, cuttings, woods, parks, golf courses, air fields, a church or a monument – and the highway itself from a study of contours, spot heights and gradient signs, summits or low points on the road. Especially at night, or in fog, the end of a long descent can be the warning of a turn 3km ahead.

Finally, link landmarks with distance. At 64km (40 miles) after joining highway 7, you will be seeing a belt of woods alongside to the West and that alerts you to leaving the highway, 8km (5 miles) further on, especially on a motorway and at the speed you are travelling you need guide points. Who knows, too, the signs may not always be lit when you reach them.

It is the interchanges that deceive on the motorway. To turn North, one goes South. Many motoring atlases include a page showing diagrams of the interchanges on a motorway. The diagrams are often difficult to follow and anyway one can hardly study a diagram while driving. However, they do indicate the complexity of the interchange, aside from showing limited access or exit. They could be graded:

  (i) direct from one highway to another
(ii) complex – more than two highways or levels.

This could help identify the interchange when the driver gets there and indicate what to expect as he seeks the right route off the circuit.

In general, European systems are less complex than those in the USA (see Part 7, especially on urban freeways in the USA).

As for other main highways, Britain believes in the *roundabout* (traffic circle) more than most. On any prompt card* mark a capital 'R' with the direction of the road you want, leaving that roundabout shown in fieldcraft fashion, eg at 12 o'clock straight ahead or 3 o'clock on one side or 9 or 10 on the other side. Using a larger scale map you can be quite precise so do not depend just on counting the turnings off the roundabout.

*See later section

Section 4: Planning Using All Map Information

Now go beyond the motorway system and *identify* the route. *Study the map to locate identification points and landmarks*. Navigate by landmarks and not by counting turnings, after deciding on the type of route you want – the fastest, or a quiet route, or a route avoiding towns – or if military, a secure route – plan so that you can best follow it.

(i) your study must ensure you can identify the roads when you reach them

(ii) you can locate and identify the landmarks by which you structure your route.

A number may identify a road but let me add a caution. *Always add a name or names, places you are likely to see on the signs*. This not only ensures that you are on the right road – especially if you add other details such as type and nature of the road or any other characteristic – but helps in following the road and diverting if need be. An East/West route across Britain is being planned; so not just A52 but A52 Grantham/Nottingham. In the United States there are many Highways 1, so if it is the State Highway 1 in New Jersey, then add New Brunswick (NJ) as a prominent place on this highway to identify it. This practice is vital on minor and cross-country routes. It also guards against confusion of numbers aside from helping the memory.

As regards the 'E' motorway system in Europe, place names are essential as the numbers are being changed, eg formerly the E3, now E17 South of Antwerp, E34 to the North to Eindhoven. Between 1985 and 1986 twelve roads changed numbers. (Unfortunately for non-Belgian motorists, place names are in Flemish in Flanders. The motorist needs a glossary.)

Section 5: Route Cards – Route Following

You have decided on your route. *Now to follow it needs a system. The system turns on memory* (see Appendix B). Before devising any memory prompt as a guide for the journey, consider:

(i) some people can memorise rows of figures; some names; others places, roads and shape of features of the country

(ii) instructions you give yourself must be simple, clearly presented and legible

(iii) any memory prompt should be compact and accessible. A complicated route card that has to be unfolded for consultation is no
good. (If the maps you use are bound in a book, insert cards at
relevant pages with main place names boldly printed on each
card.)

Any system will divide a journey into bounds or stages – as on
foot. The bounds depend on one's memory and on the distance
and on the complication of the route.

If you wanted to go from London to Aviemore in Scotland
858km, (536 miles) for a skiing holiday you would plan in bounds,
determined by ease of memory as well as where you may wish to
stop en route. There are two options:

(i) the West motorway route selected by the AA computer, which
needs a clear run on the M1 and M6 to its end and using the M74
and M73 in Scotland or,

(ii) my preferred East route: A1 to
Scotch Corner 383km, (239
miles) then at 4km (2 miles),
either proceed on the A1 (M),
then (7 miles) to the A68 *or* keep
due North on the minor road
B6275 to join the A68 across the
Cheviots, bypass Edinburgh on
the A720 from Northwest of
Dalkeith and so across the Forth
Road Bridge to M90 Perth, and
A9 to Aviemore (see **Diagram
20**). On this route the bounds
pick themselves, the first to
Scotch Corner, then a shorter
bound to Dalkeith, 214km, (134
miles), and finally to Aviemore
205km, (128 miles).

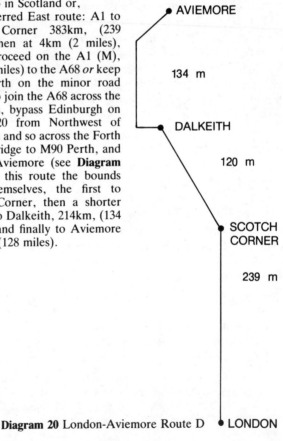

Diagram 20 London-Aviemore Route D

The route diagram shows the bounds. The OS motoring map which is referred to in the next section shows that Scotch Corner anticipates a choice 3km (2 miles) ahead.

At Dalkeith is a stage point by the junction with A6094. This anticipates the turn 5km (3 miles) ahead onto the A720. True, it is all signposted, but the short stop not only eases driving but may save the driver getting into the city traffic.

How having planned the route spend a few minutes devising your *own* memory prompt, to ensure you can follow the route without constant reference to the map.

Memory Prompt: Route Cards

The most effective memory prompt is a system of cards on which to record basic information, printed boldly and easily seen that can be referred to en route. Compile the cards from map information. This exercise makes you study the roads and *landmarks* in detail; the latter are essential where there are unnumbered or minor roads, as in many rural and urban areas. (The methodology of this book derives from an unsignposted world.)

Make the cards as simple or as detailed as you wish. Your knowledge of the area and ability to follow a route will dictate how much to include. Work up the card in the direction you have to take.

From left to right, the card can record:

  (i) place – point en route/landmark
  (ii) road number
  (iii) direction (optional)
  (iv) distance
  (v) estimated time (optional)

Then add other information, using symbols to anticipate decision points eg:

(a) a cross in a circle to indicate change from one road to another
(b) crossroads marked without a circle – you are going straight ahead
(c) exclamation mark to warn where you might go wrong – *most important* and add a thumbnail diagram if need be, eg the road forks and you indicate by an arrow the road you have to take (see **Diagram 21**).

Diagram 21 Fork

Of course, use your commonsense. Inspired reading of the map will tell you what to look for and avoid. Most major cities have roads ringing them, which may not be apparent on a smaller scale map; anticipate this and follow the road number and show also the place name likely to be seen on a signpost. Hence the names put on the card tell you what to look for.

You can also indicate briefly any anticipatory landmarks, such as the railway or river alongside the road.

It is optional whether to show both overall distances and intermediate distances.

Here is how the system operates in the three stages from London to Aviemore. (Later I will describe the systems of the motoring organisations which will give you further ideas on how to compile your own route cards).

Aviemore Route Cards
You may not consider a route card is needed for the first stage from London to Scotch Corner. It is all on the A1 or A1(M) and very well signposted. However, it is given here to illustrate the concepts. In this case the route card serves as an example of the primary route system in Britain. Anyhow, on any journey, it is no bad thing to have place names to look for, even if the route is simple and direct. You can even use such a plan on the long stretches through the United States Midwest and desert; the American Automobile Association Triptik (see Part 7) does so.

The card shows for Aviemore's Stage 1, three intermediate way points and against them mark your estimated times and later compare them with actual times. The latter operation proves especially useful – not to encourage speed but to develop an awareness of *true times* in contrast to the time some drivers *claim to take*. There can be quite a discrepancy.

The American Automobile Association gives times on its route plan. In the United States these timings are more realistic, thanks to the highway system and state speed laws. Recording both the planned and then actual times becomes a useful educator, leading to better planning and so to the allowance for more realistic travel times.

Stage 1/Card 1
First choose a start point from where to plan the route and distances. As it may be necessary to travel across suburbs and

built-up areas to reach the main road system, begin your card prompt from the first main intersection point on the road system going out of town. From whichever direction you drive you will hit that spot. This procedure can be followed for most large cities and towns with urban areas to be traversed before reaching the main highway system.

The start point for this exercise is the junction of A1 and M25 (Bignells Corner, South Mimms). This is 16 miles from the point in central London where the road officially begins. So, to reconcile the route card with the distances on the signs, start at 16 miles. (Work in miles as the signs will be in miles). Card One appears in **Diagram 22.**

Note on **Card 1**:

   (i) the letters BP against Stanford, Newark and Doncaster, indicate that these places are bypassed. Measure to a point on each bypass, identified by a junction with another road, eg Stanford BP, junct A43.

   (ii) these three places and Scotch Corner all form part of the primary route system across Britain. These names will be printed in white on green signs. Scotch Corner is a service area, indicated by a diamond sign on the map.

   (iii) the road is either A1 or the A1(M) when it becomes a motorway

   (iv) the direction is North all the way and all that is needed is North at the bottom and an arrow up the card

   (v) estimate times at 55mph average, *easily* driven on this route.

SCOTCH CORNER (Camping/caravan)	A1 (Junc A66)	239 miles	4hr 3m
DONCASTER (B.P.)	A1 (M) (Junc A630)	170 miles	2hr 48m
NEWARK (B.P.)	A1 (Junc A17)	125 miles	1hr 59m
STAMFORD (B.P.)	A1 (Junc A43)	90 miles	1hr 21m
BIGNELLS CORNER (South mimms)	A1(M) (M25 Junc) N	(16 miles)	0

Diagram 22 Card 1

So to Card 2 (see **Diagram 23**)

This card must contain more information because the route goes across country on narrower roads with many turns.

   (i) the card first shows the option at the A1(M) junction with the B6275 road, 2 miles north of Scotch Corner. The 'recommended' route, 2 miles longer, remains on the A1(M) for 7 miles and then goes to the A68. Alternatively the driver can keep due North on the B6275 and join the A68 in 10 miles. This option is indicated on the card in a three line diagram

  (ii) the map shows that the A68 must be followed carefully as it shares the road with other route numbers for certain parts of the way. Hence on the Corbridge bypass put an exclamation mark with a capital R to indicate a North turn on the roundabout on the A68. The earlier road becomes the A69 and keeps West

 (iii) a wavy line before Consett indicates that the road joins others and changes direction

 (iv) the stage point in Dalkeith is identified at the crossroads with A6094. Measure from there for the next stage

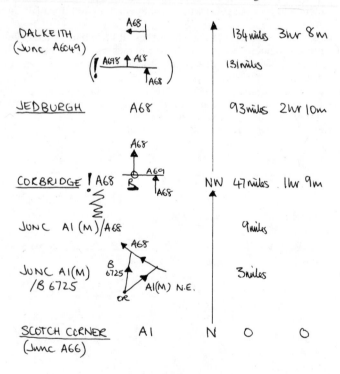

Diagram 23 Card 2

102

(v) as regards estimated times; reduce average speeds to 40mph plus. Incidentally, adding the driving time from outer London at South Mimms to Dalkeith (7 miles yet to Edinburgh) the journey, disregarding stops, adds up to more than 7 hours. Some of my colleagues claim to drive on this route from Edinburgh to centre of London in less than 6 hours but you are on holiday.

Now for Card 3 (see Diagram 24)

The last stage from Dalkeith to Aviemore. Note:

  (i) rail bridge at 2 miles shows the A702 a mile ahead

 (ii) this route bypassing Edinburgh, after 7 miles turns South joining A703 and then turns West. This is shown by a simple diagram on the card

(iii) leave the M90 at 44 miles at Exit 10 *before* the end of the motorway to proceed along the A9. Use the sign of the railway to show that you are on the right road.

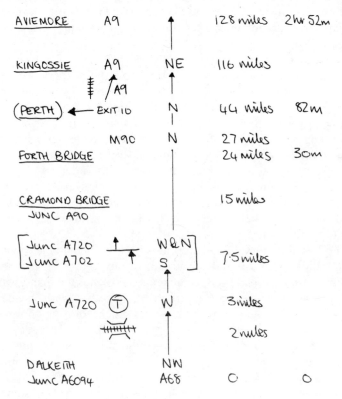

Diagram 24 Card 3

(iv) times are difficult to estimate. Allow 30 minutes to the Forth Bridge and 55 minutes to the A9 near Perth and 2 hours from there to Aviemore. This is the best way to estimate travel times where an overall average would be meaningless.

Finally, you could devise a master card to cover the three separate cards. However, for an overall memory prompt why not just use the initials – L S D P A – London, Scotch Corner, Dalkeith, Perth, Aviemore. You can fix many routes in your memory by a simple code of this sort.

Section 6: Routes from Motoring Organisations

As a follow-on to your own route planning and memory prompts, look at the guidance given by the motoring organisations for UK and the Continent of Europe. (The superb Triptik system of the American Automobile Association is presented in Part 7, the USA.)

It is the practice of these organisations to not only give the information they judge to be necessary from their experience, but this information also suggests ways to plan routes and memory prompts. The routes include the Continent of Europe, so I will deal with route following and maps in these countries as well as describing the services offered by the two organisations concerned, the Automobile Association and Royal Automobile Club.

These organisations maintain map and route advisory departments and continuously update information, as new roads are built and even numbers on the roads are changed. They both publish road maps and atlases and guide books, some of which I have already referred to.

The Royal Automobile Club prides itself on being able to give route guidance all around the world. My experience (described earlier) is that in answer to specific requests it sends out maps, with recommended routes heavily marked, together with needed leaflets giving regulations, road tolls and other motoring information (especially for overseas) and larger scale town plans. As with other motoring organisations the 'recommended' route is motorway where possible. So, in the view of the Royal Automobile Club, all that is needed is a *planning scale map* eg 1:1,000,000 and the more detailed larger scale town plans that give through routes where problems do arise.

On the Continent of Europe for *direct* routes it mostly works. The signposting is so good. *However it limits one's options.*

Computerized and other routes

In contrast to a marked map, the Automobile Association has computerized its route service in Britain and will do so on the Continent of Europe. Both at home and abroad, the AA offers the choice between the covering of long distances at speed and of seeing the country.

The decision to computerize in Britain is simple. After years of using sets of printed sheets, assembled into required routes, the AA found it needed a stock of three and a half million sheets to cope with members' needs. So it turned to the computer. It delivers a printout – two examples are shown – that give both the interval mileages between places en route and cumulative totals, together with route instructions. The computer, as in any other sphere, can only work on the information fed into it. The roads are coded into motorways, dual carriageways, open country, urban restricted and inner-city. The computer, when asked to provide a route based on time, uses the motorways and dual carriageways and avoids urban city areas as well as minor roads. Or the computer can be instructed to give a quieter route using minor roads. The programmers feed their local knowledge into the computer memory for these non-motorway routes.

The computer gives both out and home routes, which has always been standard AA practice and essential.
Reproduced here are:

(i) a section of the AA recommended 'fastest' London–Aviemore, which uses the motorways **(Diagram 25)**

(ii) in contrast, a section of a quieter route through Sussex and Kent – part of a Rottingdean/Brighton; Norwich route, past the University of Sussex. The AA had also supplied the motorway version for the same trip **(Diagram 26).**

The essence of any guide must be simplicity, whilst showing all points where decisions have to be taken – and where one can go wrong, too! As the computer must store in its memory all possible turn points for any programme it may have to give, a printout will include all *the junctions*, whether turn points or not, and so, as will be seen on the London–Aviemore printout, without necessarily being of help.

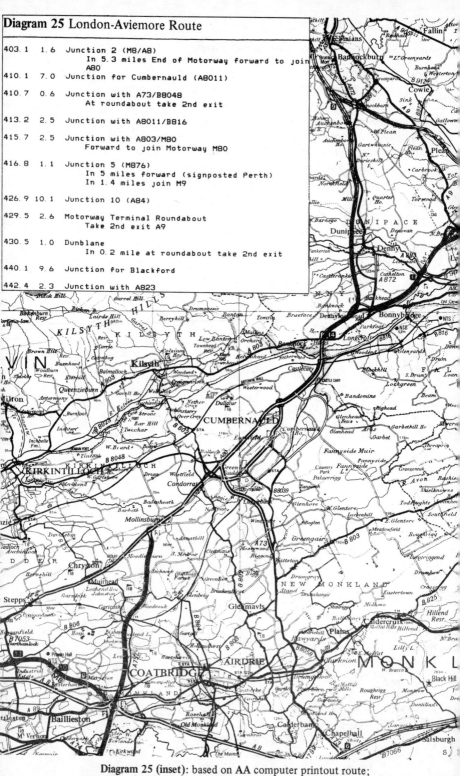

Diagram 25 London-Aviemore Route

403.1	1.6	Junction 2 (M8/A8)
		In 5.3 miles End of Motorway forward to join A80
410.1	7.0	Junction for Cumbernauld (A8011)
410.7	0.6	Junction with A73/B8048
		At roundabout take 2nd exit
413.2	2.5	Junction with A8011/B816
415.7	2.5	Junction with A803/M80
		Forward to join Motorway M80
416.8	1.1	Junction 5 (M876)
		In 5 miles forward (signposted Perth)
		In 1.4 miles join M9
426.9	10.1	Junction 10 (A84)
429.5	2.6	Motorway Terminal Roundabout
		Take 2nd exit A9
430.5	1.0	Dunblane
		In 0.2 mile at roundabout take 2nd exit
440.1	9.6	Junction for Blackford
442.4	2.3	Junction with A823

Diagram 25 (inset): based on AA computer printout route;
Map 3 Scotland related area (Ordnance Survey, 1:50,000, reduced)

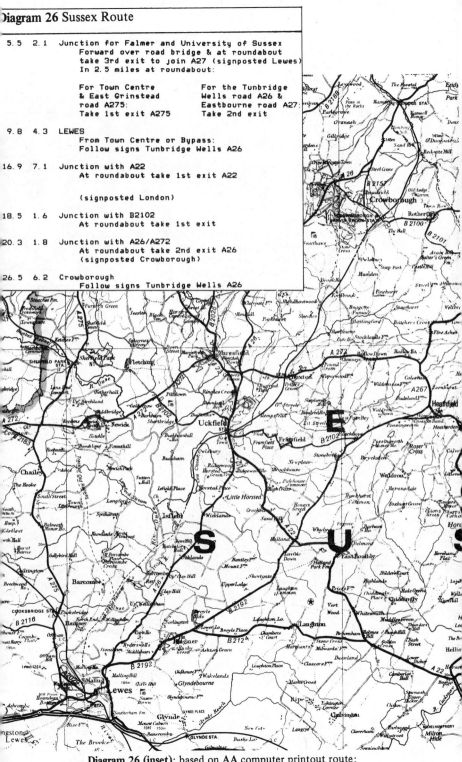

Diagram 26 Sussex Route

5.5	2.1	Junction for Falmer and University of Sussex Forward over road bridge & at roundabout take 3rd exit to join A27 (signposted Lewes) In 2.5 miles at roundabout:

For Town Centre	For the Tunbridge
& East Grinstead	Wells road A26 &
road A275:	Eastbourne road A27:
Take 1st exit A275	Take 2nd exit

9.8	4.3	LEWES From Town Centre or Bypass: Follow signs Tunbridge Wells A26
16.9	7.1	Junction with A22 At roundabout take 1st exit A22 (signposted London)
18.5	1.6	Junction with B2102 At roundabout take 1st exit
20.3	1.8	Junction with A26/A272 At roundabout take 2nd exit A26 (signposted Crowborough)
26.5	6.2	Crowborough Follow signs Tunbridge Wells A26

Diagram 26 (inset): based on AA computer printout route;
Map 4 Sussex related area (Ordnance Survey, 1:50,000, reduced)

Use of Printout

One cannot drive with a computer printout in hand. A passenger could read instructions from it – but the decision points must be given well in advance (refer again to the use of a passenger as navigator).

To use the printout effectively:

(i) underline the road to be travelled. This does not stand out from other data on the printout, where so many road numbers appear, eg underline M73, M80 and M9 where it says to join them. The printout would be clearer if there were a distinctive sign for the road to be travelled. (I have taken this up with the AA.)

(ii) *compare the printout with a map of the area*. The printout does not give a visual appraisal of the country to be traversed nor the route itself. The map also indicates where one may go wrong, as well as alternative routes.

(iii) estimate times against mileages and write them on the printout

(iv) finally, **memorise salient points** from the printout and map for your prompt card. Here the printout proves most helpful.

The Continent of Europe

The choice between the 'fastest' route and seeing the country certainly applies in Europe – especially in France; also in Switzerland and Italy.

The motoring organisations differ in service to members. The RAC, following practice at home *in answer to my request* provided 1 to 1 million map of France with the recommended route marked in my case from Calais to Lourdes in the South West of France. The RAC* 'recommended' uses all the motorway possible; first the L'Autoroute du Nord and then South West of Paris, L'Autoroute L'Aquitaine that sweeps West and South to Bordeaux. This gives more than 800km (500 miles) of motorway in the 692 miles from Calais. At the legal speed limit of 130kph† (81¼mph), which is often the minimum too for local drivers, the trip can be covered in a day, though the driver is over 850 francs poorer in tolls. (US$123 or £81.90 at mid-1986 rates.) France gives the option; pay the tolls or take the Route Nationale and pay for a hotel overnight. This decision must not only depend on cost, for the alternative Route Nationale goes, in this case, through the Dordogne. Moreover, long before the Autoroute, the Route

---

*The RAC of course will supply alternative routes and especially in Britain do provide options of routes avoiding motorway or a 'picturesque route' or for 'caravan/trailer' if a member so requests.

†20kph slower in rain and bad weather.

Nationale provided a first rate system, thanks to Napoleon III and his military successors who even planted lines of trees at the roadside to shelter marching troops on the long straight stretches. The signposts are very clear and precise. Even minor roads, D roads of the Départemente, show distances to one decimal point.

Discriminate in France. Use a 1 to 1 million (Kümmerley + Frey or Michelin) for the overall plan and the Michelin 1 to 200,000 for the region. It is difficult to get lost. The country is ideal for cyclists – the energetic can even pedal over the Route des Alpes.

The use of the Route Nationale and minor roads brings its reward. For there you will find the hostelries to stay in, and enjoy the food and wine of the region – and to see the country. When the main roads from Paris to the coast are crowded during 'le weekend' you can find quieter roads. In France maps are a good investment.

In contrast to France, there are no tolls on the motorway system of the Benelux countries and of Germany. This system provides not only fast but practical through roads in North West Europe and also South through Switzerland and Austria to Italy and Yugoslavia – using, of course, the many road tunnels through the Alps where there are tolls. Possibly, the only problem has been the renumbering of the roads and also the Flemish road signs in Belgium. But sections of the Autobahn can get very crowded and it seems the more new highways are built, the more traffic they create.

The AA has also computerized its services for Europe. Formerly booklets were provided giving page by page detail of routes plus commentary. Now each route applicant receives a computer printout for his requested destination with road numbers, distances, direction and other information. These printouts omit certain details of the home services, eg 'second turn off the roundabout' *but* they do provide other touring instructions. The AA recognises that the user also needs a map. The organisation has its own 1 to 1 million planning map for Western Europe and recommends for more detail the Michelin 1:200,000 and Touring Club Italiano. In Germany there is the RV series 1:200,000. (Reise und Verkherserlag) and for greater detail the Kompass 1:50,000. The Länder (the states of Western Germany) also issue their 1:50,000 maps.

One can request a direct or fastest route – or a quieter and scenic route from the AA.

Section 7: Route Following and Crosscountry Vehicles

Now the problems of vehicles operating crosscountry! Part 5 deals with desert navigation for vehicles that today traverse oil-producing countries using techniques developed in desert warfare as well as by new technology.

Whatever built-in aid a crosscountry vehicle has – a fixed or aerotype compass or a marine compass, or even more sophisticated devices (the magnetic component so placed that the steel and engine or wiring of the vehicle does not greatly affect it) **the navigator operates by steering marks. He looks ahead and not down!**

Certain terrain may lack steering marks. I shall look at this problem and the use of 'dead reckoning' in desert navigation. When the sun shines there is a constant guide, allowing for the passage of time. However, in most situations, the navigator can establish a steering mark on which to drive. He needs to, **for it is difficult to drive on a compass bearing**, especially one that is shaken by movement of the vehicle. To try to look down at an instrument leads to confused navigation and driving. (With a sun compass, see Part 7, the shadow of a pointer to work by is in front of the traveller.)

So from a compass bearing – even by Magnavox (Part 8) or any satellite system – or by map reading, select a steering mark. The mark must be large and distinctive. And, as noted before, objects may change shape as one nears them. A line of trees can confuse. A unique mark is needed.

Tracks can also confuse, for they may be the tracks left by other drivers looking around and getting lost, or going in another direction. Vehicle tracks obscure and replace others.

For this reason your study of the countryside becomes so important, for the contours will not change. The shape of the country remains – but again you must recognise that shape appears to differ according to your approach route (hence the accent on sketching land forms and panorama).

Again, an earlier concept of a directional framework proves useful. If you have studied the direction of a ridge, or a river system, coastline, valley or re-entrant, then even if obliged to change direction constantly, when the dust has settled, you can sight a part of your directional framework, taking a bearing and so estimate where you are or, even without the compass at least know which way to turn. The ridge runs North–South, for example, and if you proceed parallel to it you will reach a valley, cross it and turn to point 'X'. In fact given such a widely visible landmark as a ridge, you can traverse difficult country without a constant check on direction.

It is also possible to use a gap in a line of hills as a steering mark, not to aim for directly but as a reference from which to deviate by a certain distance, eg 2km East of the gap. This is all common-sense, needed when becoming engrossed in the physical task of crossing difficult country while depending on a compass that moves. *Hence, look ahead!*

There are times when it pays to get out of one's vehicle, look around to check position and plan the next bound – and brew up. You need to stop if keeping a log as in 'dead reckoning'.

At night, consult the North Pole Star and use stars as steering marks, as described in Part 3 **(Diagram 17)**.

For some reason, too many get glued to the seats of their vehicles. Yet in contrast to the motorway, there is no stopping or parking problem, unless it is unwise to stop!

Section 8: On Two Wheels

I stated earlier too many drivers know little outside their tyre tracks. The problem is simpler for the cyclist, who can more easily look around. A cyclist's landmarks would take in more country-side. To see the countryside, a cyclist has many advantages over car or truck drivers apart from keeping fit.

The cyclist will also study the contours to advantage, lacking an engine to take him up a hill. The shape of the country also serves as a directional framework. A ridge of hills runs North West – South East. The river flows South and the streams that join it run mainly from the North East and North West. The motorist should also be aware of these directions but he has less chance to observe.

On two wheels you would be using a larger scale map than for motoring, 1:100,000 or 1:200,000 which is a motoring map, too. The 1:100,000 maps would possibly show the shape of the country in coloured layers and so you can rapidly build up a picture of the country, from the river system to the hilltops.

As on four wheels, you cannot ride while studying a map. You can secure a map on a board to the handlebars but you are forced to stop to consult it. Hence, devise your own route card system, modify it to your need, and memorise it.

On a cycle one is even more aware of road characteristics. For instance, a road undulates following a river going inland into the hills. The river, having got there first, has carved a valley for itself; but man, years later, has to build the road a little distance from the river, up and down over the lower slopes, as observed in the section on contours. Hence the need to study country to supplement what is seen on the map.

You cannot use motorways on two wheels – no hardship – you can use narrow roads and tracks; further, there is no car clock to record distance (a few cycles may be so fitted, but not many). Therefore you must study your map beforehand to locate your route and seek out landmarks.

Note:

  (i) the nature and type of road itself
  (ii) rises and falls in the road and very steep hills, too
  (iii) features lining the road, whether natural or man made
  (iv) prominent features visible from the road
  (v) bridges over and under, level crossings, 'S' bends.

You depend on developing your judgement of time and distance.

Section 9: Special situations: Industrial Estates, Private Road Systems

Now apply commonsense to a common problem area, where the map may not always be of help – industrial estates, airports and private road systems. So much depends on map scale. For instance the Ordnance Survey Route Master 1:250,000 – primarily a motoring map – does not show the Upper Heyford Airfield, North of Oxford in Britain. The larger scale OS 1:50,000 not only shows the airfield but gives the detail of the runways and buildings. Even so, the road system between the buildings is not easy to follow, and the map cannot identify the building you may want to go to.

The essential characteristic of these 'closed' systems is limited entry from the public highway and limited information once inside. Which way to go? Quick inspection of the entrance show whether it is also the exit – or is there another exit? Thus you know something about the road layout; it either works its way round to the start point or to another point. So much for the obvious. Equally obvious in the case of the airfield is that there should be security personnel at the entrance to check and direct visitors.

But what if there is nobody – especially on industrial estates? You want to collect printers proofs from Bloggs, somewhere on the estate. Or collect a parcel held in a customs transit office in some remote part of an airport. There is no choice – *stop* – as in being lost. Get out of the car. Look for any plan on a notice board, list of buildings, units with some identification, eg E9, presumably a road and number; or for any other signs. What can you see about the layout of the estate? If the building you want is E9, can you see road A, B and so on?

The Principle of Straight Lines

Maybe this all sounds very simple. You may still not be all that much wiser. You may need to go round the complex and if so, do it systematically, as would the police. Work in a grid pattern – continue on the entry road, checking at intersections; then down the next, still checking at intersections. It may involve a longer drive but often en route you can see across past a line of buildings to the place you want.

Oddly enough, having reached your destination, you can still get muddled on the way out – roads blocked off, one ways and having to use another exit. Again, straight lines in the direction of the highway and turn, either at the end or earlier, if you see a well worn road way.

Needless to say, airports are not always laid out in a grid. Internal road systems conform to the shape of the airfield and runways and you may have blocks of buildings scattered round the perimeter or just outside. This is why one can lose direction – no longer are there straight lines. You may have phoned earlier for directions. What you *need to know* is the location in respect of a *fixed point*, the direction plus distance, eg on the airport South side, Entrance 2 from Highway 9, turn West 400m. Whether you receive such a specific answer is another matter.

Clearly all instructions must originate from a particular entrance which can be identified for sure. It is a long way to drive round a perimeter – and then it may not continue all the way, in view of the runways.

One problem is trying to find the right terminal building at an airport in relation to its short- and long-term-stay car parks. In this respect, London's Heathrow is a shocker. Runways and buildings were devised first. How you get there seems secondary. The time to make sure is outside at the *first signs* leading to the airport, to get into the right lane and then follow instructions from the maze of signs inside.

Even then, some desperate travellers have to drive in and then out of the airport, through the tunnel and return for a second attempt to find the right car park for the right terminal. Maybe a colour code system would help. It is very difficult, in a line of traffic with many anxious drivers behind, to slow, stop if need be and work out the message of the signs. What does each mean?

As a relevant footnote – Volkswagen at its Wolfburg factory near Hanover in Germany with building after building, spread over hundreds of hectares, has solved the problem in a relaxed way. Park your car at the entrance. The commissionaire will then say which VW *bus* to take and where to get off for the unit you wish to visit.

In many situations it pays to get out and walk, conducting a relaxed reconnaissance, but very difficult in a traffic block.

Section 10: Urban Navigation

In a way this resembles the problems raised in 'Special Situations'. This is where many do get truly frustrated. In Part 7 I will deal with this subject as applied to the USA. Even with a good map or guide it is difficult to drive and look at street names at the same time, and then recognise where you are only when it is too late. You are under pressure from other traffic when often it would pay to stop and look round.

There are two problems:

(i) locating an address in an urban or city area

(ii) avoiding city centres and traffic blocks – especially as main road systems usually intersect in city centres. Diversions may be well signposted. It depends. And then there are one-way systems, which are likely to change

Here is some advice:

(i) when seeking an address and when using a map or town guide, work from one recognisable point to another, landmark to land-mark, and add the distances between. The landmarks or reference points may be a series of intersections or junctions, all identifiable, to be followed like knots on a string. The sequence is not enough – you need direction and distance. Generally, *try operate in straight lines*, even if a little longer.

(ii) aside from reference points and landmarks to identify a route, always look for other landmarks that will *anticipate* what you have to do, eg a bridge, railway, church, which tells what to do ahead. To wait until the intersection or turn itself may be leaving it too late. As on the main highway, the secret is to anticipate, eg 1km *past fire station*, turn South (left) onto Main Street – the latter may have a road number on it – or may not!

(iii) diversions signposted 'heavy traffic' are usually a long way round. In Britain town circuits are labelled 'All Routes' which is fine but next comes 'All Other Routes' so one or two have been lost. Thus you need all the time to keep the required road identification – number and/or place name – in mind. The study of the map beforehand must identify clearly the road out of the town. Michelin maps often number turns from a bypass system round an urban centre – the French system of 'Toutes Directions'. As stated the problem is to find the right way off that circuit.

(iv) when obviously you have gone wrong then **stop** at the next place you can park. No choice! **Stop and consult.** Otherwise you can waste time, fuel and sweat trying to get back onto the correct route.

Even with the best maps and town guides difficulties arise from a mixture of the older road system and freeway-style roads that overlap and divert traffic. The town of Reading, West of London, must qualify as a place that will defy any outsider trying to reach his destination. Presumably the road system was designed, if that is the right word, by the man who invented snakes and ladders. It is not unusual to return to the start point. Reading is the cab-driver's paradise – a two-block journey will clock a mile or more on the meter. The direct way was over-ridden by planners trying to instil into the town centre another road system that included an assortment of one-way streets and diversions. For such a place it is difficult to devise a system to cope. The only clues are in difficult-to-read signs above the road; hence you must study beforehand the main places in the town and their relative location to each other. As in many towns, Reading contains natural dividing lines and barriers; in this case, the railway and the river with a one-way shopping and office complex in the centre. This at least gives the basis to work out a route system. Unfortunately, Reading is not alone in its complexity defying any route following system based on commonsense.

Section 11: Car Compass

I have left this subject until last. The car compass has a limited use. When stationary the direction for the route ahead on the map can be checked. A typical car compass obtainable from an accessory store for £12 or more (US$18) – may be fixed to the car dashboard and may be subject to variations from the metal and engine of the car, whatever the manufacturers may claim. On the other hand, the compass will show whether the car is going North or South, or East or West, which is very helpful.

It is possible to obtain a more sophisticated car compass and the reader is advised to seek the services of a specialist adjuster before fitting. This may involve more than turning two screws. A compass needs testing for variation arising from the metal and wiring of the vehicle, which has to be taken through 360°.

When the car is moving, the compass will rarely be still and to read off it you may have to wait for a steady stretch of highway before the swing is reduced enough to give a reading – in any case, not whilst accelerating, decelerating or braking.

The use of a compass for crosscountry, in a truck or four-wheeled-drive vehicle, is the same as for a tracked vehicle or across desert (see Part 5). Work on a sighting mark. Given a bearing from the map, select a point a distance ahead, approximately in line with the bearing, on which to drive. You cannot drive in the required direction just by watching the compass, which in any case on rough country will be shaken considerably. However, unlike in the desert, you may not lack steering marks.

Section 12: Experimental Psychological Study References Relevant to Map Reading and Route Finding

The methodology of this book derives from the observation of many individuals, both military and civilian and of instruction and of experience over many years – a methodology first outlined in my handbook on military instruction.

In recent years experimental psychologists have conducted studies that concern aspects of route finding, memory and, to a lesser extent, map reading. They are mostly based on small scale samples and some used students as subjects.

In the following pages are a selection of references, mainly

116

published in the *Quarterly Journal of Experimental Psychology* – unless otherwise indicated – together with a brief summary of their findings, relevant to the content of this book. I include these now, as the studies relate to the preceding four parts of this book. The methodology continues in this book but it would be also a useful revision exercise for the reader to work through the pyschological references at this stage.

The findings of experimental psychologists in *general* accord with the methodology of this book. What is probably the best known study in this field, by Pailhous, of Paris cab-drivers has already been quoted elsewhere in Parts 4 and 7 of this book.

These references relate to the quarterly Journal of Experimental Psychology (unless otherwise specified):

1 Moar, I. and Carleton, L. R. (Universities of Reading & San Diego), 'Memory for Routes' 1982, pp 389–396

The traveller encodes the locations ahead in trying to process the approaching environment. The locations of a route are remembered in the terms of the order in which they occur. Both *look ahead strategy* and the *order strategy* may be involved in the directional and distant encoding of routes. There is a build-up from routes to a spatial image like a map.

Subjects tended to be more accurate in direction of travel along the routes than in the opposite direction.

As regards route schemata, there are two stages: 1) gain experience of routes and the knowledge of spatial relations between the landmarks and so eventually a concept of a spatial layout of the complete route. 2) achieve a maplike integrated representation of the spatial layout of landmarks and routes in the area.

1a Siegel and White 1975

Subjects acquire a separate route schema for each route. When they have learnt each sufficiently, they combine them to create a global cognitive map.

Vide: Byrne, R. W. Route hypothesis -v- network retention, 1979

Siegel & White (1975) *Cognitive Maps.*

Jenkins *et al*, 1978

Alan *et al*, 1978.

Byrne, R. W. Memory for urban geography *Quarterly J EP 31*, 1979, pp 147–154 see Study Four.

Cohen, R. and Schwepfer The representation of landmarks and routes *Child Development* 51, 1980, pp 1065–1071

2 Kuipers, Human cognitives map acquisition. 1978. *Quarterly JEP*

The method to learn an unknown area is to encode places in terms of a co-ordinate frame based on the positions of prominent landmarks. Error differences also according to direction of encoding, viz forward -v-backwards.

3 Wilton, R. N. and Pidcock, B. (University of Dundee) Knowledge of spatial relations. *Quarterly JEP*, 1982, p 34.

Study experimented with the subject's ability to relate one place to another in the correct direction. The believed position turned on distance from reference point. In general subjects used one town as a reference and panned others in a relationship. The nearer the reference town, the smaller area of uncertainty.

Vide: Evans, G. W. and Peldek, K. 1980

Cognitive mapping: knowledge of real world distances and location information. *Quarterly J EP*: Human Perception and Performance 6: pp 13–24

4 Byrne, R. W., Dept of Psychology, University of St Andrews Memory for urban geography study (conducted in Cambridge).

Corners tend to be encoded as right angles. Residents estimated angles between roads by drawing. The true angles were 60°–70° or 100°–120°.

All estimates differed little from 90°, regardless of true magnitude of the angle. This adherence to the 90° corner accords with study by Lynch (1960), who found that many residents of Boston, USA, stated its parks to be *square* with *five* right angled corners!

Routes with several bends were estimated longer than linear routes – and routes within town centres estimated longer than peripheral routes – probably because of more places en route; hence more locations remembered and the longer they seem to be. Segments of route with memorable locations would tend to be overestimated.

Points with a change of bearing (needed information for navigation) were always recorded.

Large scale spatial information does not encode vector information and relies instead on heuristics (trial and error solutions) which are prone to the biases found in results. The results suggest that rather than a vector map with two-dimensional *vector* distance information, the subject uses a *network* map – a mental representation which accurately preserves only topological connectedness, ie the order of locations and turnings.

Towns are encoded in a network map, like a series of strings, each branch point corresponding to a road junction. The locations are encoded as nodes along the strings. The places where routes *diverge* are encoded for accurate navigation. Neither the distances between locations nor the angles are needed. The sequence of locations and branches is sufficient for navigation. There is the analogy of a network map like the London Tube map, ie there is a sequence of places on connecting branches.

However, to take a short cut, eg crosscountry route, one needs *vector information* and this the network map cannot provide. Subjects had a preferred orientation for drawing a sketchmap of a town. Many assume that the top of the map points to the North but subjects would be put out by having to draw the map from a direction not of their own choosing.

Probably vector maps can exist in one's repertoire of mental representations – but not the universal format for large-scale spatial information.

Further references include:

Anderson, J. R. and Bower, G. H. *Human Associative Memory*, Winston, Washington DC, 1973.

Bartram, D. Comprehending spatial information: the relative efficiency of different methods of presenting information about bus routes. *Journal of Applied Psychology*, 65, 1980, pp 103–110.

Beck, R. J. and Wood, D. Cognitive transformation of informa-tion from urban geographic fields to mental maps. *Environment and Behaviour*, 8, 1976, pp 199–238.

Cadwallader, M.T. A methodological analysis of cognitive distance; in *Environmental Design Research*. (W. F. E. Prieser, ed.), Dowden, Hutchison and Ross, Stroudsbury, 1973.

Canter, D. V. and Tagg, S. Distance estimation in cities. *Environ-ment and Behaviour*, 7, 1975, pp 59–80.

Clayton, K. and Woodyard, M. The acquisition and utilisation of spatial knowledge; in *Cognition, Social Behavior and the Environ-ment* (J. H. Harvey, ed), Lawrence Erlbaum Associates, New Jersey, 1931.

Golledge, R., Briggs, R. and Demko, D. The configuration of distances in intra-urban space. *Proceedings of the Association of American Geographers*, 1, 1969, pp 60–65.

Griffin, D. R. Topographical orientation. In *Foundations of Psychology*. G. G. Boring, H. S. Longfield and H. P. Weld, eds, Wiley, New York, 1948.

Kozlowski, L. T. and Bryant, K. J. Sense of direction, spatial orientation and cognitive maps. *Journal of Experimental Psych-ology: Human Perception and Performance*, 3, 1977, pp 590–598.

Lee, T. R. Perceived distance as a function of direction in the city. *Environment and Behaviour*, 2, 1970, pp 40–51.

Lynch, K. *The Image of the City*. Cambridge, MIT Press, Massachusetts, 1960.

Sadalla, E. K. and Magel, S. G. The perception of traversed distance. *Environment and Behaviour*, 12, 1980, pp 65–79.

Sadalla, E. K. and Staplin, L. J. An information storage model for distance cognition. *Environment and Behaviour*, 12, 1980, pp 183–193.

Thorndyke, P. W. and Hayes-Roth, B. Spatial knowledge acquisi-tion from maps and navigation, Paper presented at Psychonomics Society Meetings, San Antonio, Texas, 1978.

Thorndyke, P. W. and Stasz, C. Individual differences in pro-cedures for knowledge acquisition from maps. *Cognitive Psychology*, 12, 1980, pp 137–175.

Tulving, E. Episodic and semantic memory. In *Organization of Memory* (E. Tulving and W. Donaldson, eds), Academic Press, New York and London, 1972.

Part 5
Desert Navigation

Preface: The Problems

The desert lacks landmarks. Hence the need to rely on dead reckoning, direction plus distance. Moreover, as in the mountains – Part 6 – the terrain dictates, forcing travellers to divert from their planned route, taking advantage of any better going, as in a dried up wadi or a temporary track – not on the map – and then revert to the original route on a bearing to compensate.

Appendix D outlines a dead-reckoning exercise to illustrate what may be encountered on a cross-desert route. (Appendix D is based on an actual military exercise.)

Not only may landmarks be lacking but also maps may be vague and sometimes wrong. Features do change; repeated sandstorms will see to that. Movement of vehicles obscures tracks and creates new ones not on the map. A ridge can even turn out to be a depression, as Lt Col Richardson of the Royal Engineers (today General Sir Charles Richardson) discovered when sent forward by General Montgomery at the Battle of Alamein in October, 1942, to locate units that had been out of touch. His map certainly did not match the ground. Your task may be to reach a point that only exists on a map – there is little or nothing to show on the ground and the point you want will look like any other – just a map reference. Yet you have to be sure you have reached the right spot.

You may have to operate at night. And without twilight, or only a short twilight, you may well be caught out on a sub-tropical desert route. You may have to navigate at night and operate by the stars and compass. And judge distance, too!

Yet ironically, veteran travellers in desert terrain become so enthusiastic that they earn the title 'sand happy'. They seem to acquire a 'sense of desert'. As with direction and distance and shape and layout of country and towns, this 'sense' results from observation and memory and is a useful sense, *but it is not one a book can teach*.

It stems from intelligent observation which will see, for instance, that the desert is not flat. There are ridges and wadis (valleys – usually dried up) which a good map will show, though the map cannot show areas of shifting, soft sand to be avoided. Here, experience will warn.

Yet the desert has one plus; visibility, sometimes too far. It has the sun by day and, usually, stars by night; thanks to the clear air, many more stars than are visible above Piccadilly Circus or Times Square – a white blanket of stars!

In this Part I shall describe the Sun Compass – an older model, the Cole Universal Mk 3* – which illustrates well all the details of sun navigation.

A modern replacement has a level bubble and, for military use, is marked in mils. One still drives by the shadow cast on a gnomon, a pointer, and adjust for local, mean and apparent time.

The Sun Compass is more robust than a magnetic compass, is not affected by heavy metal or wiring and is far easier to drive by. *You can look ahead as you drive.* The Sun Compass is a very elementary instrument compared with the electronic Magnavox; this navigator belongs to the new technology and will be dealt with in Part 8. (Some are now in use with the military and police in the Middle East. The system, that gives location, direction and distance to drive on, really works. It costs £10,000 (US$15,000 at 1986 rates.) Most travellers, however, for a long time will depend on the map, a magnetic or Sun Compass and keeping a log of dead reckoning.

Study now Appendix D, the exercise on dead reckoning. The lessons are threefold.

You need:

(i) ability to *measure* and *maintain* direction, especially where lacking steering marks
(ii) accurate recording of distance – hence mileometers and tyre pressures checked
(iii) to adapt to the desert, avoid the bad patches, take advantage of good going or tracks – but then head away if they take you too far off your route. Do not assume that vehicle tracks must lead somewhere. In my experience they vanish or even double back.

---

*An even earlier Sun Compass, the Bagnold, was used by the Long Range Desert Group in World War Two – a pointer on a 360° circular plate, most *precise and effective.*

Where possible move in straight lines. Given a distant sighting point, you can deviate to avoid bad patches. But be wary – the sighting point must be unique and identifiable from wherever the approach is made.

Direction: Sun and Stars
Before dealing with any navigation instrument, note the natural, constant help in the desert – for most of the year. The sun is the guide to direction by day. You can maintain *roughly* a given direction by the sun even in the absence of obvious steering marks so long as you remember the passage of time. On an old-fashioned truck, a chalk line could be drawn across the bonnet on the shadow of the cab, or the shadow of a pointer at the front of the radiator to serve as a guide.

Without a Sun Compass, the sun will not give direction accurately. Only twice in the year is the sun due East at six in the morning, or West at six in the evening. Furthermore, there is the factor of solar variation (see **Diagrams 28a, 28b and 28c**).

Given a direction to walk or to drive, you can relate it to the sun and even travel at a fair rate across the desert simply by observing the shadow of the needle, a pointer, or of the vehicle itself.

The stars give true North at night to within one or two degrees. In **Diagram 17** are two constellations, either of which will locate the Pole Star at night. In the latitudes of a sub-tropical desert, the Great Bear or Plough is not always visible above the horizon in the first few hours of darkness, but there is the sprawling 'W' of the sky – Cassiopoea, which also locates the Pole Star from the opposite direction of the Great Bear. In the Southern Hemisphere the Southern Cross will give due South (plus or minus).

The second use of the stars is that of a skymark. As described in Part 2, if you have a bearing to walk or drive on, you can choose a suitable star about one-third of the way up in the sky, preferably one or two degrees less than your bearing. Because of the relative movement of the stars you must select a new star after a quarter of an hour.

Finally, with Astrofix, you can locate your position very accurately. The operation is too mathematical for a work of this nature. It is the job of a specialist.

The Prismatic Compass – On Foot
The compass and protractor will be the two chief instruments in

the desert. On foot, the use of the compass will not present too many difficulties, even though there will not always be landmarks to use in conjunction with the compass. But you could use a third party well at the rear as a check to maintain a straight line.

You can keep a simple log of distances and bearings, to check your position at any given moment. The problem of maintaining direction will be complicated if there are obstacles to skirt. Here, you will have to use your judgement of the distance *and time* you have gone off the original route – with luck you may even be able to trace in your detour on the map. But obstacles causing many deviations call for sound judgement of distance and direction. In principle, though, in detours keep to straight lines. (You can employ the principle in **Diagram 11**, by passing objects in the march.)

The Prismatic Compass: Use with Mechanised Vehicles
There are compasses made for installation in a vehicle. Not to my surprise, though, I hear many requests for more serviceable compasses, as the instruments tend to get shaken badly on rough going. Early on, army tanks installed fixed or aerotype compasses and today tanks incorporate sophisticated navigation systems.

The concern here is with the use in general of magnetic compasses by drivers and vehicle navigators, and the possibility of using a standard prismatic compass away from the vehicle.

Even with a special compass installed away from engine and wiring, you must check out its operation. The vehicle should be made to face in different directions previously marked out on the ground and *the deviations of the compass noted for different speeds of the engine.* Magnetic deviations alter for different directions and a deviation table can be drawn up for that vehicle.

For a tank or similar vehicle using a heavy duty compass, the operation begins with plotting on a map directions and distances, as with a ship, keeping a log and *checking the position when possible*, ie updating the logged point wherever possible.

With the special compass installed, or with a standard prismatic that must be used at least 10m (33ft) away from the vehicle with the engine switched off, employ the same basic methods:

  (i) selection of a steering mark, if possible, to use in conjunction with the compass, that includes the sun or even a cloud – but both *move*

  (ii) if it is impossible to find a steering mark, then you need to proceed about 30m in front of your vehicle, and get the truck driver to line himself up with the standard prismatic compass. Then turn right about and proceed back to the truck, on the back bearing of the original bearing. With the engine of the truck just ticking over, note the deviation for that particular bearing. Then get the driver to 'rev' up his engine and note the compass deviation with the truck at speed (it is an essential checking procedure). The truck proceeds, with you making the necessary adjustments on your compass – and halting frequently to make sure you are on the right route.

At night, whenever possible, line up your truck on a distinctive star. *Navigating a truck by a prismatic compass alone is very difficult indeed.*

The Sun Compass (Diagrams 27 and 29)
To overcome the difficulties in using a prismatic compass on a vehicle, the sun compass has been devised, having the following advantages:

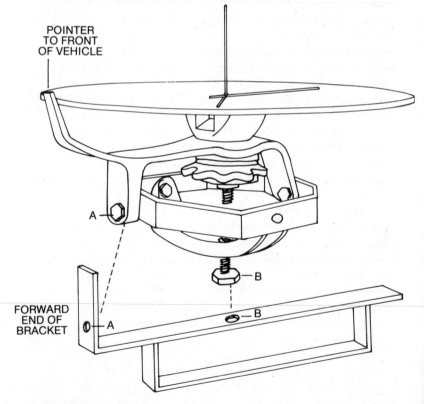

POINTER
TO FRONT
OF VEHICLE

A

B

B

FORWARD
END OF
BRACKET

A

Diagram 27 The Cole Universal Sun-Compass Mk. 3. Showing Position of Fitting to Bracket

(a) the sun compass is not influenced by the metal of the vehicle
(b) the sun compass gives true bearings – with a magnetic you must convert
(c) the sun compass is a more robust instrument, and the length of a shadow cast by the vertical pointer (gnomon) is usually long enough to be a better guide than any magnetised needle of a compass.

The Sun Compass Concept

This is described here in detail as the points made are of far wider interest. **Diagrams 28a, 28b and 28c** illustrate the principle of the sun compass. The compass depends on the direction of the shadow cast by the sun. This direction is compounded of the following factors:

1 **Latitude** The further you proceed from where the sun is overhead, the more indirect the rays of the sun. On March 21 or September 23 at midday, at the Equator, the sun will cast no shadows at all, and the angle of the sun in the sky (the 'azimuth') increases, until it becomes 90° at both the Poles.

2 **Time of the Year** The sun is overhead at different latitudes between the Tropics of Cancer and Capricorn (23½° North and South respectively), at different times of the year. Midsummer's Day, June 21, the sun is overhead 23½° North; at the Equinoxes in spring and autumn, the sun is overhead at the Equator; at Midwinter's Day the sun is overhead at 23½° South of the Equator. (In the Southern Hemisphere for Midwinter read Midsummer and vice versa.)

This apparent movement of the sun, due to the tilt of the Earth's axis is not uniform, ie in Midwinter and Midsummer, the sun appears to be standing still, hence the name Solstice for these times of the year. An examination of the Cole Sun Compass in the spacing of the markings for the times of the year, will show this apparent 'slowing up' of the sun.

3 **Solar Time** The time by the sun will be determined by:
   (a) *longitude* The Earth turns on its axis in approximately 24 hours, ie it turns through 360° in 24 hours, 15° an hour, or 1° in 4 minutes. Because of this turning of the Earth, the sun is due South in Cairo 2 hours before London, and London is 5 hours ahead of New York, etc.
   (b) *solar variation* The Earth does not travel around the sun in a circle – in the course of a year it travels around the sun in an ellipse. This causes the Earth to *apparently* spin faster at

(a) EFFECT OF LATITUDE

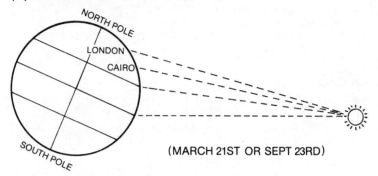

(MARCH 21ST OR SEPT 23RD)

(b) EFFECT OF TIME OF YEAR

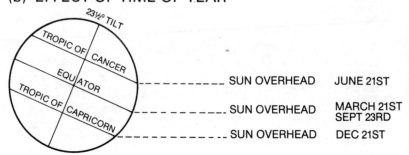

(c) CAUSE OF SOLAR VARIATION

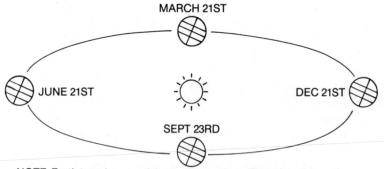

NOTE: Earth travels around the sun in an elipse. Therefore the motion is apparently faster and slower at different times of the year.

Diagram 28

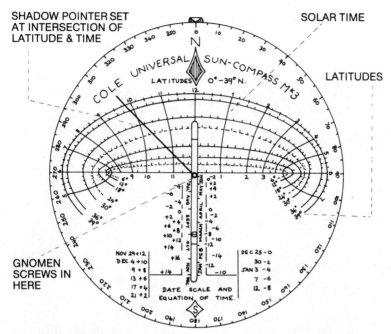

SHADOW POINTER SET AT INTERSECTION OF LATITUDE & TIME

SOLAR TIME

LATITUDES

GNOMEN SCREWS IN HERE

USE AT NIGHT

Screw second gnomen into hole at S. Then line up the two gnomens on Polaris. Drive towards star upon the bearing required.

Correction of watch for Longitude for each degree from standard meridian. Add 4 minutes if EAST. Subtract 4 minutes if WEST.

(THE INSTRUCTIONS ABOVE ARE ENGRAVED ON THE PLATE)

Showing setting for 1000 hrs on Oct 1st, at a place 30°N & 1°E of Standard time: ie 1000 hrs + 4 minutes for 1°E + 10 minutes for Solar Variation = 1014 hrs.

Diagram 29 Sun Compass Plan View

certain times of the year than at other times. The result is that, for instance, the sun is only exactly South at midday twice in the year – for every other day there is a slight variation, plus or minus.

All these points are taken into account in the construction and use of sun compasses.

How to Use a Sun Compass

Again I must go into detail, there are no short cuts. The Sun Compass described here is the Cole Universal Mk 3. (The operation of other types will be found to be basically similar.)

1 **Fix the sun compass on the vehicle,** lining it up in such a position that it is in accurate alignment with the motion of the vehicle, horizontal, and so that the sun can shine on it from all angles; yet it can be under constant observation by the navigator **(Diagram 27)**.

2 **Set the compass for the time of the year,** by moving the plate up or down the slideway.

3 **Correct the watch of the navigator for the sun**
   (a) add or subtract the variation for longitude. From the map see how many degrees you are East or West of the local standard time – for each degree East of this standard add four minutes, for each degree West deduct four minutes.
   (b) add or subtract the solar variation for the day. This will be found marked on the dial of the sun compass against the date of the slideway.

   For example, if you are in a place 2° East of standard time add 8 minutes for any day in the year. Now if on a certain day, the solar variation is plus 6 minutes, reading your watch (set accurately by standard time) at 10.00 h **(Diagram 29)**, then solar time is 10.00 h plus 8 minutes for longitude plus 6 minutes for solar variation, making the solar time 10.14 h.

4 **Set the needle on the face of the sun compass at the point of intersection of the line of latitude** (there are a series of ellipses for different lines of latitude on the dial of the compass), and the line indicating the solar time. For instance, in the latitude of Cairo, if you were 2° East of the standard meridian, on the day described in point (3) above, then, if your watch were at 10.00 h, ie 10.14 by the sun, you would set the needle to where the 10.14 line (actually you would use the quarter of an hour mark) crossed the 30° ellipse.

5 **Set the dial of the compass at the required bearing**

6 **Drive so that the shadow of the pointer lies along the needle**

7 **Each quarter of an hour, adjust the needle for the changing time**
   Note:
   (a) the procedure is nowhere as complicated as it sounds. Keep a clear head and follow the sequence. (The present day model is simpler!)
   (b) in those parts where the sun is nearly overhead at midday, the shadow cast by the sun between 11.00 hr and 13.00 hr is very short and moves comparatively fast for use from a sun-compass point of view.

128

(c) sun time has to be adjusted as well for summer time.

(d) by the use of a second pointer, lined up on the North Pole Star, the compass can be used at night. However, the range of bearings would be strictly limited to either side of true North.

Lost in the desert

An earlier section advised on what to do when lost. The same rules apply here. However, being lost in the desert is no longer a pure map-reading problem. It becomes a physical problem. The over-riding consideration is to reach a point where there is water and shelter from the sun; a question of morale. Apart from these physical considerations, note:

(a) It is essential to maintain a straight line. In a desert it is very easy to walk or even drive in circles. Use the sun, the stars, and any landmark you can see before you; even create landmarks for yourself by fixing a point 200m (650ft) ahead to make for, build a pile of stones there, then a further 200m in the same direction – more stones. On the basis of these two marks reach a third mark 800m ahead, and so on increasing the distances between the marks. After a time the direction will be fixed in your mind.

(b) Confidence is vital in the desert. Keeping a straight line with a fixed purpose will help to maintain confidence. The use of commonsense will very often indicate which direction to make for. For instance, you may know that if you go due North far enough you will hit the coast road, and so find your way back or at least to a supply of water. What you certainly cannot do is to sit down and hope for the best; *you must keep moving*, after having decided on a course of action, based on all the facts you can assemble *and write down*. **Think!**

Postscript to Desert Navigation

Having described standard procedures it is so evident that the market is wide open for the Magnavox (Part 8) or any satellite-aided instrument. Whatever instrument – magnetic compass, sun compass or an electronic satellite – an outside agency is used as with ships and aeroplanes.

Part 6
Notes on Mountain & Hill Map Reading & Orienteering

Section 1: Preface

Mountaineering cannot be learned from a book. This chapter does not aim to teach a subject to be acquired only from hard experience and first-hand tuition by walking and climbing with those who know and by learning from them.

Yet a book on map reading should refer to problems attached to operating in mountainous areas. I am concerned with those whose routes lie through mountainous areas as part of their journey or area of operation. The skilled mountaineer may find the notes of interest but this chapter is not chiefly directed at him.

In theory the subject may be divided into two parts:

(i) hill walking
(ii) mountaineering – serious! Yet the two merge, especially when the hill walking is arduous and similar conditions apply, though to different degrees.

Map reading and navigation will be complicated by physical problems, those of climbing or negotiating difficult areas of rock or scree. You cannot separate route-finding problems from the methods by which you have to negotiate your way. But it will be easier if the nature of navigational problems is understood beforehand.

I must add, incidentally, that you should not be traversing a mountain area unless suitably equipped. (See a good handbook on the subject.)

Nature of Mountain Route Finding

The obvious needs stating. The problems of route finding in mountain areas are no longer the simple problems of fixing a route from the map by landmarks, or bearings, and thereby following it. These new problems will be affected by difficulties of negotiating certain parts of a territory in which you have to operate, and by weather. The task from a map-reading point of view will not be so much as to find a route from A to B, as to find a route through the mountains which will be suitable for those who have to use it. (Leave to one side the specialised climbing of difficult rock faces.)

First, it is necessary to improve one's knowledge of landforms, contours and the configuration of the country generally. The choice of routes in the mountains will often be strictly limited – and very often the task may be just to choose between one route and another and, if military, basing the decision on tactical considerations and use of scouting sections.

Studying the Map

As described in Part 1, you must try to build up the three-dimensional view of the country from the flat printed sheet. Develop the art of mountain recognition; by a systematic study of the map know the nature of the mountain, the probable type of surface, the ease of negotiation, and the best routes up and down, plus the dangerous areas to be avoided. Precipices and areas of scree can soon be picked out to be avoided – on a map they could be ringed around with a line, so that the risk of someone descending the mountain and finding that he is on top of a 'danger' area can be avoided.

It takes a considered study of the map to determine the best way through the mountains. A short cut is not always the fastest. For instance, a few miles extra on the flat, followed by an easier route over the mountains, is far preferable to the shorter cut over a harder pass. The extra fatigue through climbing over this harder pass is far greater than any amount of walking on the flat – besides which there is a very important consideration; it is harder to keep a group together when negotiating mountainous territory than on the flat. Difficult country will split a group very quickly indeed. On the flat, people of different physical capabilities can keep together. Uphill the fit will soon be separated from the less fit, or those with a knack for climbing will forge ahead, away from their colleagues.

All these considerations must be taken into account when studying the map.

Nature of Tracks in the Mountains

Many of the routes through the mountains will consist of following streams up to a pass and descending the other side by following streams the further side of the pass.

Diagram 29a Zig-zag Nature of Mountain Tracks

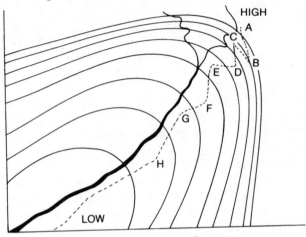

NOTE: As slope becomes steeper, path crosses contours at more oblique angle

In **Diagram 29a** is an example of a path following a stream up into the mountains. Lower down, the path will be fairly direct, bending fairly easily. As the path becomes steeper, the bends become more acute, ie the bends in the track at B, C and D, are more acute than those bends lower down at F, G and H. As the track reaches the summit of the pass it will usually bear away from the stream altogether and flatten out – then it will descend again in a similar fashion.

The nature of the rocks will govern the distance of the track from the stream. The stream will have carved a deep bed for itself, and the track will be above and away from the stream. It will often be found that there is a well-defined track both sides of the stream. If both tracks are equally well marked on the ground it can be assumed that both are as easy, or as difficult, as each other. There is a common illusion that, when one is climbing the track one side of the stream, the other side of the stream looks easier. This is often the result of the fatigue in climbing affecting eyesight and judgement. A third route could entail walking through the stream itself if the rocks are not too slippery.

Using a Compass
Because of the zigzag nature of mountain tracks it will be obvious that a compass cannot be used for *maintaining* directions in the

mountains. *The chief use of a compass is that of locating position* – when there is good visibility (often a mist or the clouds will obscure landmarks). Furthermore, the use of a compass is complicated by the fact that many mountains contain rock that will disturb the magnetised needle. *Local knowledge is essential.*

Descending

The descent presents problems and danger. A common experience is that of going down the wrong side. Often at the summit the visibility is nil, and even with a compass it is difficult to judge the route to descend. If there is a ridge from the summit leading to a lower level from which it may be easier to find the route down, then that ridge should be followed, even though the point it brings you out at may be a little way from your rendezvous.

If you find that you are going down the wrong side of a mountain, it may prove safer to go up again *towards* the summit, and down the correct side, rather than work your way round the side of the mountain. This statement does not contradict the principle set forward in the next paragraph, that of 'keeping height'. This principle is applied in usually different circumstances.

Keeping Height

Earlier in the book, this topic was discussed briefly on contours, the principle being to use the contour lines themselves as though they were tracks on the mountainside.

In **Diagram 30** are marked two routes from A to B. The apparent direct route by a straight line means in practice that one must climb from A to D, descend from D to E, climb from E to F and down to B. Apart from the fatigue of climbing, it is difficult to maintain direction if one has to constantly climb and descend. In climbing from A to D it would probably be necessary to zigzag considerably to reach D. The descent from D to E would entail more zigzagging, and so on.

It is easier to maintain direction by keeping height, ie follow the dotted line on the map ACB. Very often the task in route finding can be simplified to the following of a given contour, which, if followed for a certain distance, will led to a stream which leads down to the destination. Clearly this process may be rendered difficult when it is too awkward walking on the side of a slope, *but if possible* this method of maintaining direction will be found very useful. Keep the principle in mind.

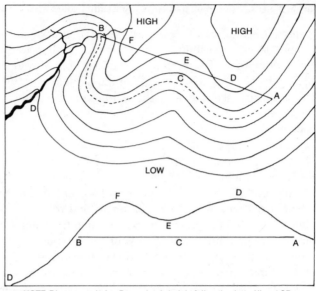

NOTE: Direct route is A to B to maintain height follow the dotted line ACB

Diagram 30 Keeping Height

Estimating Distances and Time

It will be found that there is a great tendency to underestimate the distance to be covered in mountainous areas solely from a map. The map cannot show all the twists and turns to be followed, or all the difficulties of climbing. It will be necessary to multiply all the apparent distances on the map by a certain factor depending on the nature of the territory. If you must compile a timetable in such an area, add *a minimum* of half an hour for each 300m (1,000ft) you must climb.

Judging distance in the open will be found *deceptive* in the mountains. The peak of a mountain which looks a few kilometres away may be a whole day's climb, and while from the peak of one mountain it may seem 'a stone's throw away' to the next peak, yet it would probably take hours to descend the first peak and nearly another day to ascend this neighbouring peak. You must revise your standards of judgement.

These notes on mountain map reading include further advice for those operating in mountainous areas:

(i) if any form of track has to be constructed going up a mountain pass, then make the track cross the lower contours at right angles, and the higher contours obliquely.

134

(ii) a track will be flatter that crosses a series of streams at the heads of the streams, than halfway up the streams.

(iii) respect scree or loose slates.

(iv) plan the route so that you do not get stuck on a mountain pass for the night – unless the situation compels it. Descending rocky passes at night is not the route to a long life!

(v) if a mist descends, and you are in doubt, either wait for the mist to lift or climb up out of it to a point from which you can check your position. Before descending make sure of what is below.

Driving in Mountainous Country*

So to a related subject – driving in mountainous areas.

The earlier description of how a track ascends a valley, holds for many mountain roads, especially on the Continent of Europe. Many of these roads are very old. They were originally built for horse traffic, and achieve easy gradients through a system of endless hairpin bends. The twisting nature of these roads often confuses one's sense of direction and must be taken into account when judging the distance by road between two places. It may prove necessary not only to double the distance as the crow flies, when working out a route between two points, but also to allow for the climbing necessary, the descents in gear, and all the other problems of hill driving.

It must also be noted that no map can give every bend on a road, unless you are using a very large scale map; but the map maker usually does his best to indicate the nature of such roads by inserting as many bends as possible. Apart from this, you must use your commonsense, and appreciate that unless the road is very exceptional and is carried on viaducts or taken through cuttings and tunnels, then by the nature of things the road must wind considerably – even if it just seems to be following a valley towards its head, until it reaches the stretch of flat at the top, before dipping to the other side. True, in the Alps, more and more tunnels are replacing the older routes over the top – but there remain many roads that conform to this description and present the same problems in many parts of the world.

ORIENTEERING

Froebel preached learning through play. The sport of orienteering

---

*Note: as a point of interest, in really mountainous country, a right-hand drive vehicle comes into its own on a 'left-hand' road.

undoubtedly teaches people to read maps, choose routes and follow them.

An orienteering event is held on a circuit. It is often very hilly, identified by a series of map references – control points – which have to be covered to complete the course against time.

The orienteer has a map; not an ordinary one, but one specially prepared 1:20,000, 1:15,000 or even larger scales. The sport produces its own maps based, though, on the Ordnance Survey. The orienteer's map includes a wealth of detail; contours at 5 metre intervals and even symbols for density of forest, or a stone wall, or a fence – any factor that may affect progress.

From a personal point of view, some maps contain so much detail that they can confuse. However, to make the shape of the country stand out, I would mark distinctly certain contours at wider intervals in order to get a better picture of the area the user is going to see and recognise and have to cross. Also exceptional features should be circled lightly, eg the knoll, not apparent on a standard OS map, but important in the landscape.

Before setting off, the orienteer copies the controls of a master map onto his own map. Problem: the route to take. The usual option is between the direct and maybe difficult route with climbing and descending that can fatigue, and a longer route, also easier to locate by landmarks. It is difficult to run on a compass bearing. This will be a 'rough' bearing until the final approach when it will be a 'fine' bearing. **The orienteer must work from mark to mark.**

The sections in this book on contours, the shape of the land, prove most relevant, as well as sections on route finding and navigation. Significantly, navigational advice and even a diagram or two in orienteering books resemble the theses of the original manuscript on which this book is based (see note on copyright). Aside from the map, the other item needed by the orienteer is the lightweight compass, the Silva, described in Part 2. Speed is essential. The compass gives direction and helps to locate position; the orienteer has to identify features, and obviously needs to memorise basic details. In this, he must be systematic, noting key features that identify a route and what will be seen.

As a final observation, excelling in this sport demands more than navigation. The truly physically fit have the advantage, not only in covering the terrain, but in decision taking. They have more options and probably are mentally less stressed.

Part 7
Route Finding & Map Reading in the United States: An Appraisal

Section 1: Preamble: The Problems

This part outlines the special factors in the United States route planning and following, and shows how map makers and motoring counsellors tackle the problems that arise in a country, which extends diagonally, North-West to South-East, coast to coast, more than 3,500 miles.

The distances in a country, where one state, Texas, is bigger than France (and France is the biggest country of Western Europe, taking more than 200 Michelin 1:200,000 road maps to cover) – whilst the whole of Great Britain could be lost twice over in the State of California – present the United States map maker with a headache.

How much legible detail can be covered on a sheet of paper?

Over to Rand McNally, whose maps are found at gas stations and stores throughout the USA. Open a book of maps, published by the company, entitled *Road Atlas*, sub-titled, *The Perfect Trip Planner and Traveling Companion*, that goes into Canada and Mexico. One page alone truly highlights the problem. It gives distances, 6,889 of them, all in one page, between the main places in North America, in 84 columns crossed by 84 rows, where the reader, no doubt with the aid of a magnifying glass and a ruler can pinpoint the mileages: Miami, Florida, to Seattle, Washington – 3,273 miles; or from Providence, Rhode Island to Wichita, Kansas – 1,554 miles* just two of the six thousand and more mileages on a page that must surely qualify for a distinguished mention in any book of records.

Consult such a chart at a wheel of a car or even by the light of a motel room. One needs the sharp eye of the proof reader. Unfair to Rand McNally? Not entirely! The problem stems from a series

---

*Greater, incidentally, than the total mileage in a month of the average British motorist.

of the inter-related facts that make life difficult for the map maker and map reader in the USA.

(i) the United States is vast.
(ii) in this space the people of the United States work in thousands of cities and then live far out in 'streets' and country areas that stretch for miles.
(iii) unlike Europe, the railroad system has declined and public transport systems vary – very good in cities like New York or San Francisco, but otherwise in the USA you fly or you drive, especially drive. No country in the world so depends on the car and gasoline.
(iv) cars demand roads.

And here is the contrast, the contrast summed up in a quote from William C. Sunier, Chief Cartographer of the Triple 'A', The American Automobile Association: 'We can send a member two thousand miles across the United States and lose him in the last ten or twenty miles. There he will be getting out of his car to phone Aunt Ethel in her cabin to find out how to get there – maybe minutes away!'·

The magnificent interstate highway system crisscrosses the country; Highway 80 runs from San Francisco to New York. But when you get off the highway, you may be into poorly signposted country and urban areas, where one place looks like another and the address is in the thousands on a street with no apparent beginning or end, which may, in the middle, disappear into the woods to reappear on the further side, necessitating a hopeful detour.

Whereas in main cities like New York street numbering is well organised, in many localities, including Washington D.C. or Houston, Texas, the number is inconsistent, depending on the lot numbers and early surveys. However, the stranger is helped at intersections in main cities and urban areas by the number of the next building on the street under the street name on the signpost.

To add to the problems, in a country area you may well wonder . . . are you in Gainsville, Mainsville or Plainsville? They all look alike and all have a West 4th Street!

Confusion arises notwithstanding the signpost at the town limit announcing name and population, especially in areas where one place runs into another.

One must sympathise with the map maker. For the map maker has at the same time to cope both with the problems of *size and of detail.* Rand McNally tries to solve the problems in one way; the Triple 'A' approaches them differently, as you will see.

Part 7 examines both approaches. Rand McNally is primarily a map maker. The Triple 'A' is more involved in solving the problems of navigation, or route finding, for its members, even to the point of having tourist counsellors whom members can consult before setting out. The organisation is very aware of the basic attribute of a map. *It must be clear.* There must be a sharp limit to the information put on a sheet of paper. The task of a map maker is to select. And if the area to be depicted crowds with detail, then one must proceed from a summary map to a local map, the latter of sufficient scale to show the details *simply and clearly.* On the way travellers have regional, state and county maps.

Basics

First, though, a basic observation. The principles of navigation and map reading outlined in this book hold good for anywhere on Earth. You find your way by reference and identification points – landmarks. You proceed from landmark to landmark in a given direction – North, South, East or West – for a given distance – using the highway or track available.

If you are lucky enough to get out of the car and walk in national parks or over tracks in rural areas, you will find guidance in the other sections on route finding. But mostly I will be concerned with the problems of wheeled navigation. Again the principles outlined earlier apply: **navigation begins before setting out; study first; then drive.** You cannot drive and read a map at the same time. You need a system to appraise the relevant details from the map, plan and then follow the route with fewest snags.

Having studied the area to traverse – the more that is known of it, the greater the chance of locating landmarks and guidance if you want or need to divert and the more likely you will choose a better route – you come to the highway system and the beginning of road wisdom. Learn how the system is laid out and the way highways and roads are numbered.

First there is the multiplicity of highway types, each with its own numbering system, identified by signs as shown in **Diagram B**.

(i) US Interstate
(ii) US Federal
(iii) State and Provincial
(iv) County and local

Next, the system depends primarily on numbers in its signposting, more so than in Europe. Destinations on the signs will be chiefly to the next county seat or principal city, rather than to a distant destination; the same highway number can go from the Atlantic to the Pacific. So you need to know intermediate places that will tell you you are on the right route and also that *you have turned in the correct direction to join that highway*. Hence, the earlier advice in this book, to link the highway number with place or places to identify it for sure – especially as there are different numbering systems side by side, eg interstate and local.

There will be examples of some freeways where a sign just announces a distance to a highway number. So you must know how the numbers are arranged and where the highways lead. Sometimes the road has a name, eg the Santa Anna Freeway in LA. But just as streets and cities are numbered, so are the roads, *North to South being odd numbers and East to West even numbers*. In the newer *interstate* network the *lower numbers* begin from the *West* Coast. The *older state highway systems* begin the *lower numbers* from the *East*. True, you can follow a route by numbers, which is fine if you begin and finish on a main highway. But numbers not only mean you must learn where each highway and road number goes to, East and West, North and South, but they also add to the problems of memory. It is easier to confuse numbers than place names, and I will show a system to aid memory in this respect.

Another problem arises from the signposting on freeways that intersect urban conglomerations. Here what is seen announces half a mile to a street number or the name of an unheard of street. In theory one should be able to identify these exits from a local map, but good local maps, as the AAA emphasises, are not always easy to obtain.

Landmarks
Another problem on main highways and freeways stems from lack of identification/reference points and landmarks. Now this is a problem the American motorist shares with the European who uses the new motorways. For so often they lack external landmarks – and they disorientate. Roads on and off so often reverse direction, aside from the effect of the highway to isolate the driver from his surroundings. It is a self-contained world.

In contrast, older road networks relate more to their surroundings. They played a part in the life of people before the motor car. Accordingly, they have landmarks which help the traveller to find his way.*

On the other hand, roads in urban areas and small towns also lack unique landmarks, as does that route leading off the main highway to Aunt Ethel's log cabin, referred to by the AAA Chief Cartographer. How to find your way in such an area I will come to later.

How does the motorist cope in the USA? He keeps very much to the main highway system, to the freeways and toll roads; these can get very crowded and are certainly no place to relax.

One object of being able to use a map is to get off the main routes and find quieter and maybe more picturesque roads.

How then does one tackle route finding and map reading in the USA?

The Triple 'A' System

Let me describe the AAA approach. For this will illustrate both the problems and solutions. It will tell you a great deal about maps for motoring in the USA.

At the outset the AAA recognises that one works from the general to the particular. A motorist has a long journey. The master plan is made on a smaller scale map covering a large territory, possible the entire USA; then as detail is required, one uses a regional map of a larger scale, and then a state map of even larger scale and finally, if needed, an even larger scale local map. (It parallels the method described in the chapter on 'wheeled map reading' but with more stages.)

The AAA also locates a route by a series of strip maps, *Triptiks* – made into a booklet. I will describe this service in a later section. First here is the concept of an operation from smaller scale maps to larger.

Exercise: to send a motorist from the East Coast, New York, to Hollywood, California – and see the country on the way. There will be many stages to follow and maps to consult. It is a step-by-step operation.

---

*In Britain there may be a pub on an important corner. One can plan a route by a series of pub names – from the Red Lion to The Bull or King's Head – and the traveller can be sure he is on the right road. There may be churches, road junctions, bridges. Railroads and rail stations make useful landmarks. Significantly, the Triple 'A' does not include railroads on its maps – though in Europe these are useful landmarks.

141

Stages; USA: (i) an overall map of the USA for main planning of 90 miles to the inch: 1 to 7,500,000

Region (ii) The AAA supply three regional maps to cover the route from New York to LA:
(a) North Eastern States and Provinces
(b) Central States and Provinces
(c) Western States and Provinces
varying from 25 miles to the inch to 40 miles to the inch. They show the main highways and more important connecting routes. They cannot show every detail. This would confuse. The maps show the main routes. And, in fact, it would not be desirable to do more, as the attempt by many maps one buys at a gas station to provide both distance and detail results in a confusing map. The makers are too ambitious . . .

State (iii) The third stage in the AAA system is the state map. The traveller began by consulting the USA and then the regional map. Now to look at the larger scale map of the state. The AAA has a map for California, 1in to 7¾ miles or 1 to 500,000 approximately. Now this map shows the road system in far more detail.

Local (iv) But even then the AAA is obliged to go to a fourth stage. As an inset on the state map the freeway system in downtown Los Angeles is shown on a scale of a mile to the inch and the same holds for San Diego, or downtown San Francisco, and then for various national parks on a range of scales.

Now come two more stages. The Automobile Club of Southern California provides a map of Los Angeles and vicinity giving 4½ miles to the inch, and extending from the West of Malibu to Palm Springs and from North of Lancaster to San Clemente, setting Los Angeles into context. Then the club supplies a larger scale map, ½in to 1 mile approximately of Metropolitan Los Angeles, with even larger scale insets. However, even so the road information is limited, otherwise it would be illegible.

YET ANOTHER MAP: STAGE 5
There are addresses to visit. **So you need yet another map, apart** even from the AAA maps, in yet finer detail. Buy a Rand McNally map, published by Mitock Publishers Inc., entitled *Street Map of Los Angeles*. And this is a larger scale map than any so far – 1in on

the map equals 0.68 miles on the ground. You may suspect another map sponsored by the Optical Association to encourage eye testing. On the Venice Waterfront in LA more than 50 street names squeeze into an inch or two, looking like lattice work.

The map maker is wise enough to present also a more general map (as an inset) *Los Angeles and Vicinity*, one inch to 5.7 miles, showing the relative positions of the main places from San Bernardino to Santa Monica, with the joining road system. You have Beverly Hills and the Hollywood Freeway. Turn over to the lattice-work street map, and there search for your destination in Hollywood.

The map maker has tried so hard to cram in every road and even street number on one side of the paper, but pity anyone looking for a back street in the industrial estate of Culver City where you will find streets blocked off – a fact that the map cannot show!

In principle a general plan map is required with main places and main roads and then larger scale page after page of local detail. It is confusing to show both the main layout and the detail on the same sheet. Literally thousands of blue lines cross each other and some disappear into canyons with a name in the tiniest of type.

The AAA states that it has a minimum type size for its maps. Such a practice is sorely needed. The AAA's belief in clarity and simplicity is nowhere better shown than in the Triptiks, described in the next section.

The maps I have referred to, whoever the publisher, all derive from two sources:

(i) Department of the Interior: Geological Survey
(ii) Department of the Army Corps of Engineers

(See the note at the end of this part for details of maps and where obtainable. They are the best buys I know of in the Western world, and are highly recommended).

You have the maps or know where to get them. For local details maps you must wait until you reach the area to obtain them. Not always easy; aside from the services of the area automobile organisations, to find your way around you need more than the usual gas station map or the one at the hotel.*

———————————————————————————————————————

*Note: members of the AA in the UK can obtain information and guides of the Triple 'A' in the USA by applying to the Overseas Route & Touring Information Unit, Automobile Association, Basingstoke, Hants. RG21 2EA.

The AA also publishes *Discover AMERICA* (£7.95) and *Destination USA : East* and *Destination USA : West*, both at £1.

Section 2

AAA Triptik

For a journey anywhere in the USA, the AAA Triptik supplements the map. The Triptik comprises a series of route strip diagrams, with maps and information on the reverse, made up into a booklet to cover the required route. I shall show examples.

The Triptik helps you to plan your route; then to follow it. It serves as a memory prompt. You can devise your own memory prompt from it.

Request a guide from NY to LA (as in the exercise) or from Pittsburgh (Penn) to Austin (Texas) and the AAA assembles the booklet of strip diagrams to form the route. The first takes you from New York into Jersey and then to Delaware on Interstate 80, and so on in stages of 50 to 100 miles in the East, to longer stages of 200 miles as you go West taking you from coast to coast. The highways to follow run down the page, with place names, other highways, exits all marked and distances – plus a commentary. Example: from Colby, Kansas, to Denver, Colorado, the Triptik states: 'rises in elevation from level prairies to rolling range lands, devoted to agriculture and cattle ranches. Route has good alignment and grade'.

So no problem! Also the AAA estimates 4hr 5min for the 221 miles of the strip. There cannot be any hold-ups, if you drive at the legal limit.

The Pittsburgh to Austin booklet proceeds in the same fashion, using some of the same sheets as NY to LA, early on and then turns South and South West.

The AAA Triptik, however, gives more than the direct route. *It presents options* – without being requested! Thus the AAA includes in its booklet not only the direct route on Interstate 70, West of Denver, Colorado, but offers as an alternative the tour of the Rocky Mountain National Park and then goes South through the Indian Reservation, Four Corners Monument to the Grand Canyon. After all, if you want to go fast from coast to coast you take the plane. In a car, see the country.

Altogether, thirty-seven sheet route diagrams are sent to cover direct and alternative routes across the USA.

The strip diagram shows the route, intermediate places and mileages and details of what you will see. On the reverse is the map of the route you take, scale 1in to 36 miles – for the Triptik must be used in conjunction with a map – not only that area but also the overall view on the AAA regional map so that you can link one with the next and plan! As a memory aid, underline places en route. A Triptik informs about the road and grade and even warns of dust storms.

Triptik 86 1–C Walsenburg, Colorado to Cortez is reproduced in **Diagram D** on page 36.

Taking advantage of the options presented by the book of Triptiks from the AAA, you have diverted from Denver, Colorado, south to Walsenburg to take the scenic route West to Cortez, a 269-mile mountainous stage. The relevant page from the Triptik book is shown in **Diagram D**. This passes the wooded Mesa Verde National Park with its score of large canyons, and the cliff dwellings in the caves. Durango is the southern end of US 550, a spectacular leg of what is known as the Million Dollar Highway, North to Outray and Grand Junction (on another Triptik strip). All the details quoted are on the reverse of the Triptik, as is the area map – an extract from which is in **Diagram E**. A Triptik may also show on its reverse a town or city plan, such as that of Grand Junction, or it may show a plan, as of the Mesa Verde National Park.

Note on the Walsenburg strip **Diagram D**:

   (i) the North pointer on its side, ie the route travels East–West
  (ii) the mileages, forward and in reverse
 (iii) the numerous camping sites, denoted by a wigwam symbol
  (iv) the caution as regards trailer traffic
   (v) the estimated time of 5hr 46min, an average speed of 46 mph. This gives a measure of the gradients, compared with the 50 mph average on Interstate 70 from Denver to Grand Junction or 53 mph from San Bernardino to LA (the same average from Dallas to Austin, Texas).

Finally, as a memory aid underline or list on a card the key places en route: Alamosa, Monte Vista, Del Norte, Pagosa Springs, Durango.

So far so good. Your maps and the Triptiks take you across the USA. You still have the problem, what happens when you get off the main highway, even with all the local maps?

Off the Main Highway

   (i) You are in a dispersion of lookalike urban areas and centres: Gainsville, Mainsville, Plainsville, all with a McDonalds and a gas station. Roads intersect and lead to places unknown. This is the *urban problem*.

(ii) Your destination is on a rural street, numbered in the thousands, indifferently signposted – a street that runs for miles; or you want Aunt Ethel's log cabin on the narrow road into the hills, where the AAA confesses members can get lost. This is *the rural and country problem*.

In all situations ask: what information have you got? Start with the obvious, everyday practice. The local map may be crowded but it usually includes a gazetteer. Gainsville is E8 – but this can cover a wide area. Within E8 you want a focal point, a main intersection, clearly marked on the map. This will become a *measuring point*. It is also the approach point to your destination, for when you seek instructions you want them to refer to a point of this nature, as well as to the direction and distance.

The map gives prominently adjacent highway systems. You will be travelling on it, so you must first identify the turn from it and then define the direction, road and distance from that turn point. Measure on the map with a ruler or even with thread that turn point to Gainsville intersection (all place names and roads are fictitious in this example). Now plan:

(a) leave Highway 7 at Oak Heights junction, 12 miles South of High View interchange with Highway 610.
(b) East of Canyon road, 10 miles to intersection of Beech and West, in Oak Heights.
(c) fork South 12 miles to Gainsville intersection. (See **Diagram 31**)

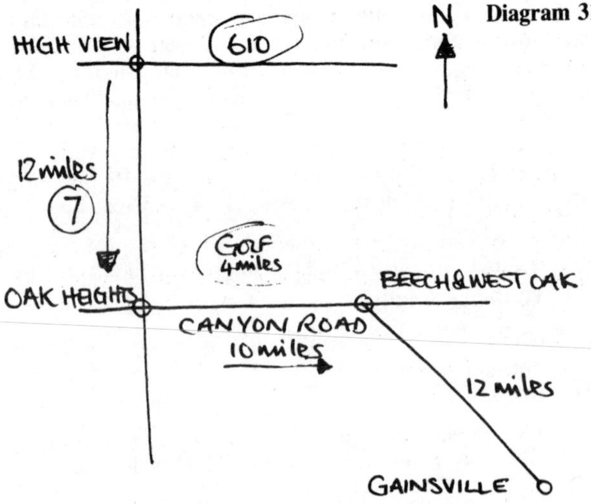

Diagram 31 Memory Aid

This goes to what is termed the approach point, as near as possible to the final destination. The final miles depend on the information needed from one *identifiable* point to another, as in Part 4 'Special Situations'. (For ETAK technology applied to this and similar problems, see Part 8.) The plan from one identifiable point to another, plain commonsense as it may be, can now be augmented to ensure that you follow it without hassle or getting lost. You always need to identify the route and know you are on the right road – and know soonest when you are on the wrong road. I have outlined a procedure you can adapt to many situations, even to the log cabin. But to ensure you follow it:

(i) you want landmarks you will pass on the way or see from the road. You know you turn in the right direction from the main highways because you can see the lines of hills straight ahead. From Canyon Road 4 miles East of the highway you should see a golfcourse on the North side of the road. *But be wary.* The Metropolitan Los Angeles map of the Automobile Club of Southern California shows 142 golfcourses in the area covered. Gas stations, of course, are out – unless there is a distinctive name, ie not the brandname of a fuel. However, rivers, bridges, airports and hills all serve. They help to identify the route. On a long feature, a street that runs for miles, **a landmark is needed, unique in relation to its surroundings.**

(ii) But you need distances to be sure. You know you are in Gainsville because your focal point there is 12 miles South East from Beech and West in Oak Heights. At 22 miles it would be Plainsville. As stressed in Part 4 of this book, *use the neglected mileometer of the car.* It alerts instantly if you are going wrong. Then you can follow the procedures of 'What to do When Lost' given in Part 4. **Stop!** Think back to last point you knew to be correct. The rest has been outlined earlier.

You may need this procedure on the trip to the log cabin. Obvious as it may sound, you must always move from one identifiable point to another and so when you are stuck you think back to that recognised point. On the rural routes you are up against very indifferent signposting and roads which do not always appear on maps. There is no magic answer. The more systematic you are the less you will waste time and fuel. It is a case of establishing landmarks, reference points and *distance*, the use of an instrument on the car dashboard.

Section 3

More on Route Planning and Following for Long Distances

[1] *Plan the rest stages*, where you can also plan the details of the next stage. Shorter stages are easier to memorise and follow.

[2] Think in time as well as distance – fundamental to all route following.

The last point is often easier in the USA than in Europe, thanks to speed laws and enforcement on the highways. However, when the freeways get into urban areas you may become involved in congested parts of the day – one reason for learning a quieter diversion *and* for using a map! However, in general you can plan time as well as distance.

The Rank McNally *Road Atlas of the USA; CANADA; MEXICO*, provides two useful introductory maps of the USA, to form Stage 1 of any plan. One map shows the **United States Interstate Highways** and the next a more detailed **Mileage & Driving Time Map** of the USA:

> Dodge City to Oklahoma City, 253 miles, 5hr 40min driving time . . .
> Chicago to Toledo, 232 miles, 4hr 45min . . . and adding some distances, Los Angeles to Houston, Texas, 1,540 miles and 32hrs of driving.

No-one guarantees that you will make it in precisely 5hr 40min from Dodge City to Oklahoma City but the time provides a guide. You know what you can do in a day and so plan the breaks.

Memory and Peripheral Vision – and Route Finding

Once on the way you depend on memory, not only for numbers but for the shape and layout of the country gleaned from the maps and Triptiks.

What should you remember from a check list of any plan?

(i) main place names
(ii) highway types and numbers
(iii) places either side of the highway
(iv) directions – North, South, East and West
(v) distances in miles and time
(vi) landmarks, especially those that precede a change of route. Anticipatory landmarks, vital in making sure you change correctly from one highway to another and leave the highway at the right exit.

148

If you can retain information from points (i), (ii) and (vi) you will be doing well. These are essential.

Aids to Memory

How can you fix numbers in your mind to avoid confusion? The simplest method is to interpose a word between the numbers. The sequence on the route card from Grand Rapids to Terre Haute is not difficult to learn (see **Map 5**).

131 (US highway)*
94 (Interstate)
41 (US highway)

But you can fix these numbers more firmly in your mind with relevant link words:

South 131 (US highway)
West: direction Chicago 94 (Interstate)
South: Terre Haute 41 (US highway)

The link works give direction at the interchanges as well as aid the memory.

Follow a similar system where there are connecting highways on the interstate system ending, for instance, in 5s, as in Los Angeles, and so have to memorise a sequence: 5; 405;. 605. You will be surer if you add the freeway name, such as San Diego for 405 and San Gabriel for 605. But not all highways and freeways have names and so you must find a relevant place name or direction to act as a link word.

Directional framework

This book emphasises that the key to navigation is to know what lies either side of the route. The psychological researches in Appendix B show how too many drivers dispense with peripheral vision. Because they know only the road they are on, raises problems when it becomes congested, or when they have overshot the turning or taken a wrong turn or even become lost. Three steps widen the vision and aid memory:

(i) construct an area grid system. For instance, in Pennsylvania fix a quadrilateral in your mind: **Philadelphia : Harrisburg : Williamsport : Scranton.**
  Then fix firmly the direction of the main land feature in that part

---

Note: alternative route, 196 interstate.

of the USA, the Allegheny Mountains. Not only do they govern the direction of many roads but also they act as a direction reference when a driver turns onto a main highway. You know when you are going in the correct direction if the mountain range is on your left or right, depending on the route taken. Note: in this context you *can* use 'left' and 'right'. Within all this system, you now locate places you have to go to and routes to take and can repeat this in many areas of the USA.

(ii) construct a grid for an urban area; instead of the one road, followed by another road, there is a pattern. Take four highways that form a box. Then you can get onto the box and take the road you need off it.

This is the system of the Paris cab-drivers, as established by the French psychologist, Pailhous. In spite of having to cover an area of at least 200sq miles, in practice the Paris cab-driver managed to find his way by a very limited number of routes structured by a series of grids, related to basic points. There would be a central grid and an outer grid – a box within a box and roads linking the two.

It is possible to extend the quadrilateral fixed for Pennsylvania. Add another to the South of the original grid and one to the North and so extend the range. Short cuts will then come with experience and intelligent map reading, plus **confidence** gained from mastering route finding. You can divert from the blocked freeway and go mile after mile along older roads and even through urban streets. Just study the map to note the older highways that newer systems have replaced. Even without the map you can sometimes work by the direction of the sun and commonsense.

The interesting and reassuring point is that although legends abound of people who were looking for San Diego ending up in Las Vegas, in fact most people find their way in the USA. It is just that too many get on the same stretch of highway at the same time.

The map plus commonsense can be so useful.

Survey maps in USA

Maps in the USA are based primarily on data supplied by the Geological Survey via the Department of the Interior. The Corps of Engineers: Department of the Army, maps conservation projects, such as dams, watersheds and land conservations. Even

Map 5 Grand Rapids to Terre Haute (AAA, 1″ equals 30 miles)

the map at the gas station traces its origins to the work of these two bodies.

The maps are kept up to date by Aeronautical and National Oceanic Surveys, as well as from local informants who note roads under construction for an organisation such as the Triple 'A'. The basic map of the USA is the 1:24,000 (1in equals 2,000ft). This is a very detailed map indeed. If you were developing property in a locality you would need such a map. Then the Department of the Interior publishes a series of 1:62,500 (approximately 1in to the mile), again most detailed.

From the motoring point of view, there is the 1:250,000 series, which is a major source map for the AAA.

To show how many maps are involved to cover the USA; for the State of Florida alone, more than 600 maps are needed on the 1:24,000 series compared with 14 of the 1:250,000, some of which extend into neighbouring states. The Survey also publishes a 1 to 1 million series, the Jacksonville sheet taking in parts of Florida and Georgia; and it publishes a mobile sheet including parts of Alabama, Florida, Georgia, Louisiana and Mississippi.

A 1:500,000 map, about 8 miles to the inch, that covers Florida, shows counties, location and names of all cities and towns, most smaller settlements, railroads and township and range lines, rivers, streams and other water. The topographical version of this map also shows contours in brown, and highways in purple, as well as national forests, national parks, wildlife refuges, Indian reservations, built-up areas for cities and county boundaries. From the motoring point of view the 1:250,000 and the 1:500,000 prove most useful within the state.

For overall planning, there is the AAA regional (1in equals 24 miles, 38.6km or 1in equals 40 miles, 64km) and USA maps, the latter being 90 miles to the inch. Larger scale local maps vary in quality, as commented on in Part 7; AAA maps are clearer than most.

The Geological Survey prints a USA map of a slightly larger scale of 1 to 5 million, 80 miles to the inch.

The maps vary in date. As stated elsewhere in this book, one of the first points to look for in a map is the date of its last revision. In a country of highway construction this becomes very important indeed.

The **grid** on USA maps is the **World Geographic Reference System** that locates any point by two letters and four figures. The

grid originates from a point at the South West, from where to measure distances to the **East** and then to the **North** . . . to the **right** and then **up** the map.

The maps described in this section may be obtained from:

> Branch of Distribution
> US Geological Survey
> Federal Center
> Denver, Colorado 80225
> USA

National Park System
The National Park System is well mapped by the United States Geological Survey and the reader can do no better than obtain from the Denver address of USGS an *Index to USGS Map Coverage of National Park System.*

Besides this system, three goups of related areas exist – Affiliated Areas, the Wild and Scenic Rivers System and the National Trail System.

National Parks, such as Yellowstone National Park, are tinted in red on the conventional topographic maps with National Memorials, such as Joshua Tree NM, in yellow. Parkways and scenic trails are shown. The published National Park Series of Topographic Maps cost US $3.60¢ per sheet. Some parks require more than one sheet. The Conventional Topographic Maps cost US $2.25¢ per sheet for 7.5ft and 15ft maps, US $3.60¢ per sheet for 1:100,000 scale and 1:250,000 scale maps – very good value indeed!

Part 8
The New Technology

Introduction

Electronic technology has guided marine and air navigation since the 1940s, using DECCA, LORAN, VORDME and similar systems that identify position by relating it to fixed points from where signals are transmitted. Air travel, where planes can follow each other in a queue over the Atlantic at five mile, thirty second intervals, could not have developed without such guidance systems. However, there has not been the same urgency to take advanced technology into land navigation. But, for a world in a hurry, and a world with a belief in technology, it becomes inevitable. The story, though, had a fortuitous start.

Section 1: Satellite

Preamble: The Satellite

It began with the Russian Sputnik in 1957. Quite by chance, two American scientists from Johns Hopkins University, George C. Weiffenback and William H. Guier, found that they could determine the satellite's orbit by using Doppler shift observations. The Doppler effect is similar to the variation in sound coming from a moving source, like a train whistle – in this case the variations were in the reception of radio waves from a moving satellite. The radio waves are constant but the ground receiver gets varying signals as the satellite moves, and by counting the cycles at intervals of time, the satellite path can be tracked.

From this chance discovery came the United States Navy Navigation Satellite System, a series of satellites, to be called the TRANSIT system, that transmitted signals on stable frequencies. Using the Doppler effect their orbits could be tracked. *Positioning the satellites fixed the observer's position on the ground.*

Two networks track the satellites, OPNET in the USA and TRANET around the world.

For the operator of a satellite tracker unit, the TRANSIT system is simple. In one minute a ground position, accurate to within 100m, can be established by a single pass overhead. The system needs only a single whip antenna for operation. Then the scientists found what could be done by setting up two receivers one kilometre apart. Satellite readings taken over 72 hours enable one to fix a position on the ground to within 30cm (1ft) – less than half a metre. The principle of location from two base points has long been used in navigation, eg DECCA or the ELT fitted to small aircraft enabling them to be found, incidentally, if in trouble. However, *the accuracy* of satellite location marks a considerable step forward, as explained in the text. Such accuracy may be hard to believe but is fact. It is all a far cry from the theodolyte and triangulation. The surveyor, the map maker, the engineer, the geologist, already enjoying the benefits of the airborne camera, can now pinpoint positions in areas with few, if any, identifiable features – desert or arctic wastes. This is aside from use in standard surveying and mapping.

Satellite systems have made possible a simple, accurate, simultaneous *timing* of two distant points on the Earth's surface. Formerly such an operation would have been very involved – and the timing not as accurate.

Satellite systems, moreover, normally contain in their Earth-based receivers the means of recognising the true shape of the Earth, which is not a sphere but is flattened at the Pole and has bumps, enabling the system to calculate in *Geoid* measurements, with the necessary compensations.

For more than a decade the system has identified precise positions of oilwell heads and rig moves in areas with no external reference points to identify their location. One is measuring in the middle of nowhere, to within a few inches.

Experts in this field, Racal Positioning Systems, have operated this technique for the oil companies of the type manufactured by the Magnavox Corporation of California, its MX1502, which is also used by the military as a satellite tracker.

The other vital development, of course, has been the microchip, enabling satellite data to be recorded and utilised on equipment no bigger than a standard TV set – and at faster speeds.

The satellite has transformed navigation, first at sea and in the air. Now it is being used on land, and it can be predicted that it will dominate the new technology.

For it:

(i) gives location
(ii) is not subject to cumulative errors of dead reckoning, as is any system *based solely on compass plus distance.*

True, it is limited:

(a) in urban highrise areas
(b) in dense jungle with tree-overhang, though a vehicle equipped with a telescopic antenna to project above the trees could cope.

In urban highrise areas a system (described later) based on compass, dead reckoning and updating of position by map matching, will be mainly used.

The military regard the satellite as vulnerable and so demand a backup system. The British Navy also navigates by way of two megahertz frequency stations, transmitting a code of pattern like DECCA, in the North Sea and Eastern Atlantic.

The military also use inertial systems, the gyro-compass and North-seeking gyro instruments, whose operation cannot be affected by a hostile agency. I shall deal with this later.

But for the vehicle operator and driver in open country, guidance will come from the sky. In urban areas there will also be local radio beacons, signals at fixed points, as begun by British Telecom, or coils under the road, as used by London Transport, to identify positions and track movements. However, such operations are limited; the satellite is universal.

TRANSIT, though, is limited. There can be long intervals between satellites whose inclination above the horizon is big enough to measure. A new American system, GPS,* will take over (see later section on Magnavox MX 1612). GPS will function well in the urban areas.

How far the claims of German researchers that satellites – or ground stations – will one day control the movement of every car, even starting or stopping them through junctions as well as directing their routes – remains very much to be tested and proved. For the limiting factors in all this technology are the instructions that can be fed into the system, determined both by

---

Note: Global Positioning System (GPS) is expected to be operational by the 1990s. The space segment of GPS will consist of 18 satellites operating in 12-hour semi-synchronous orbits in six inclined-orbit planes at an altitude of about 20,000km. This configuration has been selected in order that a minimum of four satellites will be above the horizon at any time anywhere on the Earth's surface.

the sophistication of the microchip and computer, and by the software programme. Even the successful Magnavox MX 6102, already in use across the desert, has had to update its technology. Users claimed the Z80 chip could not store more instructions. The manufacturers claimed it was not the chip but the software programme, and it has now been revised. Yet its demands are modest against the needs of a system to regulate and control all vehicles. There is also the basic problem of continuously updating the map and road information – including one-way systems – on which any system depends.

In this new field of vehicle navigation, one needs to retain the critical faculty. Publicists, TV and press reporters make claims; manufacturers present demonstrations; but it is very difficult, mostly impossible, to get a trial over a route one chooses. It is already prepared.

In this Part 8 I shall describe what is actually in operation or, if still a prototype, how it works. I shall try to present an evaluation of the system described, though somewhat dependent on manufacturers' claims. In one case, ETAK of California, the makers declined to answer specific questions and I have had partly to reconstruct how their system must work.

In describing how the technology works it is necessary to deal with specific proprietorial systems. I have tried to be representative of manufacturers in the field; Magnavox, which has established a reputation for engineering, with systems already in operation and working comes first.

Review of Systems

Magnavox 1502: Satellite tracker and locator.
The Magnavox 1502 tracks satellites. It locates position. Motorolla of Tempe, Arizona, makes an equivalent unit.

The unit is the size of a TV set, incorporates its own computer and standard keyboard and works off a 12 volt battery. It is linked to an outside antenna, the size of, and looking like, a partly-folded rotary clothes drier that can be seen in any suburban garden. It costs US$50,000–75,000.

Here is how it works: you are in an office of the School of Military Survey in Berkshire, England. On the VDU are the details of satellites that have gone over earlier that day. A second instruction gives the programme ahead. The usual satellite frequency is 2 to 3hr.

Now instruct the computer – *give position*. The VDU reads: North 51° 27″ 3′ West 1° 17″ 3′ **plus** a third unexpected dimension: Height 160m. Your location is in *three co-ordinates*. For the remarkable attribute of the system is to give z as well as the x and y co-ordinates. Until now navigation systems have only given x and y. Latitude and longitude are also different. They are geocentric, Earth centred co-ordinates, WGS 72 – spheroid.

As an aside on this question of latitude and longitude measurement – the *geodetic* will replace UTM (Universal Transverse Mercator) grid systems in many parts of the world, especially for the military. UTM grids can pose problems where adjacent systems do not match. Satellite navigation gives latitude and longitude – and height. *You can programm for grid if wanted.*

The military evaluate the satellite tracker Magnavox MX 1502 as a translocation module of extreme accuracy. It will be adapted to the Global Positioning System as it comes into use in the 1990s.

I have started with the static locator. Its technology leads to satellite-operated navigator units. So to the first operational land navigator, the Magnavox 6102 which leads the way across deserts and featureless country.

*Magnavox MX 6102: Across country and desert navigator

The Magnavox MX 6102 fulfils the three criteria needed by a feasible navigation system. It gives:

(i) position – it locates
(ii) direction – it has a compass
(iii) distance.

There are vehicle navigation systems being devised, some of which I will describe, which score on points (ii) and (iii). However, to operate on all three counts *needs an outside agency*; in this case the satellites. Systems which claim to be completely self-contained with no outside agency are limited, by definition.

From a critical view the MX 6102 has two pluses:

(i) it works
(ii) quite aside from the fact it is already used by the military and

---

*On a personal note, before writing I found how the system commanded respect amongst senior personnel of rival companies, so much so they did not contemplate making a competitor. I also had a critical military evaluation by those putting it to hard use.

police forces in the Middle East, it makes no extravagant claims as regards accuracy; no more precise than within 300m of one's destination, which is enough in the desert – the rest can usually be seen, unless tucked away in a wadi. There are three versions, a standard; a waterproof, which partly meets military specification; and finally a mil spec.

A standard unit, one off costs £10,000, US$15,000 (1986 rates). The MX 6102 can operate off TRANSIT and a new model will later use GPS. The system comprises:

(i) a basic unit, which can be portable – if need be, strapped to the back of a soldier. This weighs 5.4kg standard or 7.2kg military.
(ii) a fluxgate compass
(iii) an antennae on vehicle
(iv) speed sensor, operated from gear box or speedo cable, that gives distance – this can operate by electronic pulse or mechanical clicks (see later the observation on wheel slip).

Before operation, the compass has to be calibrated for the vehicle, when loaded, by being taken through 360° in both directions. Calibrate, too, for local magnetic variation and time. The unit includes a very accurate atomic clock.

The unit is placed in the vehicle where there is the least magnetic interference. One can test the vehicle by marching round with a hand-held magnetic compass. The wiring of the vehicle or a touch of the brakes will affect the compass.

One calibrates for:

(i) axis of the vehicle
(ii) axis of the compass

The fluxgate compass takes account of the dip due to the magnetic field and to the rise and fall of the road.

The system will give readings either:

(i) map grid, taking account of magnetic variation
(ii) latitude/longitude – satellite data WGS 72 (World Geodetic System).

The system gives two sets of information:

(i) dead reckoning from the initial position speed and head of sensor, 1 to 2% error on distance travelled
(ii) updated position by satellite, TRANSIT to within 200 metres. (With GPS will be accurate to within 50m.)

In operation, the heading and distance are updated every half second. Magnavox are aware that dead reckoning unchecked can take a vehicle off-course. Hence they can fit an alarm system which sounds when the vehicle nears its destination so alerting the driver, a similar system to that used in a yacht. When driving, two indicators show whether the driver deviates left or right – so he should steer a course in between.

The system can also adjust for hard or soft ground. The atomic clock has to be set for the time zone. It is very accurate, using atomic vibrations as the standard of time, and is essential for use with the satellite.

The user can feed forty-nine places into any programme on the way and the computer will give headings and distances between. Hence the very busy Z80 microchip. Naturally the desert forces drivers to deviate and then it becomes necessary also to give fresh instructions to the computer.

Finally, as with the Magnavox MX 1502, this system gives a third dimension, *height*, which enables contour information to be used as a guide in route finding.

Military Users' Evaluation

  (i) The system gives location, bearing to drive on and distance
  (ii) it gives intermediate points
  (iii) errors occur because of wheel slip, even though the system can be adjusted for rough or smooth going. This affects measurements from the vehicle's own distance system
  (iv) it is influenced by the mass of metal, wiring and electrics.

Magnavox Comment
  (a) the manufacturer, aware of the problem of wheel slip in the sand and rough terrain, contends that what is lost uphill is balanced downhill. There still remains slip on level going. However, as no claim is made to greater accuracy than within 300m, the problem must be set in perspective. Moreover, the receiver is updated on each satellite transition.
  (b) as regards magnetic influence of heavy metal, if the vehicle is loaded with ammunition boxes or weapons or similar heavy metal, then take the vehicle through 360° and calibrate afresh for deviation. This will take account of its load, although this system, like any other using a compass, must always be influenced by other vehicles or nearby metal objects – and any electrical fields. This is inevitable. All manufacturers are only too well aware of this problem and design special compasses to counteract 'outside' influences.

Magnavox MX 4400

Looking ahead to the 1990s, when the GPS satellite system becomes fully operational, a new positioning system, the MX 4400, has been developed, which gives a position to within 2 to 3m, five to six minutes after observing.

The 4400 is the forerunner of a new generation of positioning devices made possible by GPS. It is not for precise urban survey work, boundaries between property or administrative areas, but it will locate the routes of pipelines, farm boundaries, forestry work, pylons and give positions in the desert or in the Arctic and Antarctic. Even with the present (1986) limited number of GPS satellites, the system can already function at the times of the day when the 'satellites are in the window'.

The receiver weighs 7.25kg (16lb), draws 20 watts and can be taken virtually anywhere. The whole pack, though, weighs 22.7kg (50lb) – fine for a vehicle but less so on one's back.

It aids navigation by giving a position when needed, but it does not replace the MX 1612, the terrain navigator, or the MX 1502, which is primarily a satellite tracker, aside from giving position.

In the following sections I will describe the non-satellite car navigation systems. They are mostly in prototype but should be on the market in the late 1980s. They have been the subject of considerable publicity. I shall attempt to assess their feasibility.

Section 2: In-car Systems

Compass, Dead Reckoning and Map Matching Systems

Most of the electronic, computerized vehicle navigation systems, introduced in the 1980s, operate:

(i) *for direction* – by compass, usually fluxgate, coils of wire in a container sometimes no bigger than a man's hand

(ii) *for distance*, which, in conjunction with direction, enables dead reckoning – by sensors attached to non-driving wheels measuring the outside distances travelled by the tyres, as in the case of Plessey.

The sensors have another function. The use of one on each side of the vehicle gives direction, from the difference in distance travelled by the wheels on either side. The sensor differential may even tell the computer that the vehicle has made a *real change* in direction as indicated by the compass – or whether the compass

161

swing results from metal or electrics from a passing vehicle or from other outside influence.

This principle of sensor differential, with its automatic check on compass direction, is used in many in-car navigation systems, including Plessey PACE; Philips' CARIN; EVA (Blaupunkt) in Germany; ETAK in the USA.

Most systems operate with a digitized map. (See later on digitizing methods.) The capability to interpret the data on the map, the signs for rivers, roads, contours, different highway types and any other symbol, so that it can all be processed by a computer, has transformed not only navigation but also map usage and production. The map is now more flexible; it can be enlarged or reduced at a touch of a button. It can even give three-dimensional models and so solve the problem in seconds of where one place can be seen from another on that model – given the provisos outlined in the earlier section on 'Intervisibility' (Part Two).

Although hardly ever mentioned in the publicity – if at all (maybe the designers are more scientists than navigators) – unless the system has an independent method, of location, as the Magnavox 6102, by satellite, or by radio beacons, then everything turns on:

(i) **accuracy of the original map** – in particular how **up-to-date** – and even last week's map in an urban area may be dated because a new road was constructed or a traffic system altered

(ii) **the accuracy of the digitizing.** Now strangely, although the Ordnance Survey in Britain and the Geological Survey in the United States will digitize maps and have areas already processed, many navigational device manufacturers do their own or commission this work. Digitizing has become a backroom or cottage industry – possibly because the navigational producers want only road information (see the section on digitizing at the end of Part 8).

One cannot stress too strongly the need for map accuracy and ensuring that all relevant detail is selected and digitized. For many systems, Plessey, Philips' CARIN, ETAK included, depend on map matching* to update and correct positions, ie movement and position on the ground must correspond with that on the computerized map. The computer should correct positions if they

---

Note: *map matching ability has been enhanced by the increased power of the computer processor, thanks to advances in the microchip memory.

deviate, eg follow a turn. All depends on the detail provided on the original map. Is an alleyway, a turn to a car park or to a factory, shown on the map? Any system producing a map display on a VDU and directing the driver to the next turn ahead must depend on the map corresponding to the ground.

This problem is dealt with at length because it is of prime concern to the system designers; note how companies like Philips and Plessey are looking for an outside agency, eg satellite or radio beacon to augment their systems.

The following sections describe some typical systems that are coming into use.

Plessey PACE (see **Photo 3**)
The intriguing attribute of the Plessey PACE car navigation system is the price, £500 (US$750) for the hardware, mostly for the compass. This compares with £18,000 (US$27,000) for a gyro-compass and twice that price for a North-seeking gyro. The software, the cassettes with map information, are extra; price to be determined.

The designer's achievement is a very clever electronic compass that copes with the tilt of the road, uphill or downhill magnetic field declination and with the surrounding hardware of the vehicle and other metal influences. Yet the whole unit fits into a box 22.8cm by 12cm (9in by 5in).

The distance sensors, located on the brake drums, measure the travel of the outside tread of radial tyres, however inflated. The system does not depend on the car's own measuring instruments.

The Plessey PACE shares with the Philips' CARIN the need to programme one's position on the map before starting and another map reference for the destination. The start position must be accurately recorded, as, in any method of dead reckoning to establish position, errors are cumulative. This is a problem. Incidentally, the manufacturers claim that in the years ahead users will only need to programme the computer with a postal code for where they are and to where they are going.

Facing the passenger seat – at least in the UK because of legal requirements – there is a computer operated VDU that displays a map of the road system. As the car travels an arrow points to its location on the road. It is small but visible and even corrects itself if the car takes a turning where the computer is at first unsure which road it is.

Directly in front of the driver is a digital unit giving instructions, a bearing, other information, and will indicate '100m ahead turn left'. The manufacturers aim to incorporate a voice synthesizer so that a verbal instruction can be given to the driver. It is not always easy to read instructions on a VDU. There may be strong light in the driver's eyes.

The computer works on the shortest route but it can be instructed for variations. Plessey claim to be accurate to within 2% of distance travelled.

Does the system replace the need to understand maps and navigation, as the media have suggested not only in respect of this system but all others? The answer is 'no'. Those who are good navigators will profit by the system. Some indifferent navigators may benefit but not to the extent the publicity would have you believe. In any case, you will have to be able to read a map accuratelv to give an eight-figure map reference where you are at the start and an eight-figure map reference of your destination. The map display on the VDU will mean most to those who know maps.

Plessey PACE Evaluation
The Plessey adaptive compass, the brain of the system, represents a great advance in nagivational technology. Significantly, it is also made for use in aircraft and marine. In a vehicle it is sited away from the engine and electrics – usually in the boot (trunk). Calibration takes 10 seconds and a minimum of knowhow. It needs a weekly check.

Although the compass can be insulated from the car, external factors influence it – other vehicles, highrise buildings with steel rods in the concrete, or electrified railways. These factors are usually temporary and the system corrects itself later. Adjustments are needed for local and short term variations of the Earth's magnetic field. An accuracy within 2% on journeys greater than 10km is *claimed*, assuming positive and negative errors cancelling each other out. (Claims of any manufacturers always need independent testing.)

The whole system turns on accurate programming of the computer, giving *eight-figure* map references for start point and destination. It is then subject to errors of dead reckoning and hence its designers will look for radio beacons or other outside agencies to update position in a future Plessey system. Philips'

CARIN, a similar system, will look to satellites for the same reason.

However, especially in outer urban areas with crisscross roads and in poorly signposted rural areas – all areas of difficult route finding – the system has a lot to offer.

The system is more fully used if there is a passenger to operate the computer and VDU map display. That is where the computer and VDU are sited. The driver on his own must rely on the instructions displayed on a rectangular display panel in front of him, eg where to turn. When voice synthesized the system will benefit. *This is a consideration that affects all similar systems.* Moreover, it would be a great advantage for any driver to have consulted a map first to gain an overall view of the route. He can then anticipate instructions and check on them too. Can one take it for granted that the system works correctly every time? Not in my experience; not only of the computer but also of the operator!

CARIN (Philips)

A very similar system to Plessey, giving the user a route from start point to destination. Hence I have not described it in great detail. It is understood that future models will have a more sophisticated compass and Philips will introduce a compact disc laser player to store maps as well as to play music. Philips claims the ability to combat influence of metal on the existing compass by use of a combination of metal sensors placed round the vehicle.

Demonstrations of the system were certainly impressive, with the constant reminder to programme the computer correctly at the start point. The manufacturer is very aware of the problem of location and, as previously pointed out, will look to an outside agency, such as satellite.

Philips has developed its UK operation through the programme of urban data recording, aimed at covering the entire country.

ETAK (California, USA) (see Photo 4)

ETAK slots into a ready-made market in the USA. As pointed out in Part 7, problems begin when a driver leaves the main highway

---

Note: ETAK may be introduced into Britain. It will be interesting to see how a system that works best in the grid pattern suburban layouts of the USA, enabling constant self-correction to its augmented dead-reckoning, fares in the differing city and town layouts that often go back into history – market and town squares, narrow curving streets close to each other, now superimposed by one-way systems. In the USA, Boston, Mass., an old city within later developments, presents problems.

for the urban complexes of poorly signposted roads and streets, which lack landmarks and stretch for miles.

ETAK belongs to the group of car navigation devices based on a compass plus sensors that not only measure distance but also direction by differential travel of the non-driving wheels on opposite sides of the car.

However, ETAK differs in an important respect. The name derives from the Polynesian navigational concept of the canoe being stationary and the islands moving round and past the canoe. So, *in a car it is the map that moves*. The driver is at the centre. It is an electronic map giving a vector* display on a 11.4cm–4½in or 17.8cm–7in screen, of the road system ahead and key landmarks. The more important the road, the brighter on the screen. An arrowhead in the centre gives the vehicle position, the map pointing in the direction of travel. The map rotates and shifts about the arrowhead as the vehicle moves. The driver can change the map scale, so bringing into focus the smallest street if need be. As the scale is reduced the area covered enlarges and certain details disappear as on any map.

To find your way, feed into the system your destination street address or a street intersection. The moving map in front of you shows the road system ahead, which is read like any other map. Choose the route from the display. As you follow it the map moves and from wherever you are the *view* ahead on the ground should correspond with the map on the VDU, with the moving arrowhead giving the position. Direction and distance to destination are continuously indicated. A blinking star on the map marks the destination.

How does all this happen?

The system includes:

(i) an electronics unit, installed in the car boot (trunk), comprising three circuit boards
(ii) a solid state compass, half the size of an audio cassette, fixed either under the car roof or on the rear window
(iii) sensors on the two non-driving wheels.

Plus

map cassettes for the area in which you are travelling (scale from ¼ to 40 miles to 1in). Each cassette covers twice the area of a standard street map one can buy at a gas station. Another indication of the distances

---

*See note on raster and vector digitising of maps.

covered is the statement that one cassette will take in a third of the Bay area of San Francisco.

ETAK costs US$1,395 or 1,595 for the hardware according to screen size and US$20 to 30 per cassette plus US$100 to 200 to instal – a procedure that takes between two and three hours – presumably at an authorised vendor. The system's memory is taken care of by a .12 watt trickle charge from the battery, even when turned off. The ETAK publicity states you have only to switch on the car engine and up comes the map on the VDU to show where you are and the direction you face – but not if the battery goes flat or is disconnected – or, most importantly, not if the system has not been initialized, a point I shall come to.

'The system', says the manufacturer, 'requires no programming or external connection source and does not accumulate positioning errors – no matter where you start or stop, the Navigator will continue to display your current position'.

It is quite a claim.

For, in fact, the system depends on the car driver at some stage entering a computer-recognised start position into the unit – the easiest way to go to the nearest intersection of two streets, say, Powell and Market in San Francisco – and feeding this information into the computer. Only the first three letters of the street name need be entered; thus the map is set. The system will be kept up to date as the vehicle reaches other intersections or turns on a distinctive pattern in the road, eg a prominent 'S' bend that will match the computer map. This constant update is needed for accuracy – for the system is prone to the problems encountered by any dead reckoning device, where it may accumulate errors over a 30-mile straight stretch if there are no points to update it. Presumably the driver takes part in the update. (Updating was one of the questions put to the manufacturers on which I did not receive a specific answer and can only reconstruct what must happen from write-ups and other sources.)

ETAK and similar systems all turn on map matching. Messrs. S. K. Honey and W. B. Zavoli of ETAK, in a paper to the NAV 85 Conference in York, England, underlined the technique needed in map matching, where the key to system performance is proper updating.

For with any dead reckoning system, positional errors accumulate proportionally to the distance travelled and to the inaccuracy of the sensors.

Hence Plessey in Britain, Philips in the Netherlands and other manufacturers look for an outside agency, satellite or beacons to supplement and check the compass and sensor date – but this ETAK has set its face against. The company is resolute in its belief that the system must be self contained with no outside agency; it claims that LORAN or satellites are not practical in urban areas. Instead ETAK operates on what is termed 'augmented dead reckoning'. This is its method of continuous map matching. Drivers mostly keep to roads. By comparing the vehicle's track with the digital map, so the company claims, the navigator eliminates the accumulated error from dead reckoning. Turn a corner and the navigator makes a new update. Erroneous updates destroy the positional accuracy and may cause the system to become lost. And here is the problem for anyone trying to evaluate the feasibility of the ETAK system, which claims accuracy to within 50ft, and not becoming lost within 120 miles, on average – and then taking only 20 seconds to correct.

The problem is one of total belief in the claims. (ETAK declined to answer specific questions, in contrast to other manufacturers. It sent plenty of publicity material and later write-ups, including one in *Navigator*, to which I am indebted.)

Part of the problem is the publicity – *with no outside agency you can switch on the engine and know where you are.* Does ETAK then have a direct line to the Almighty? Magnavox uses satellites. Plessey, Philips and other systems need to be programmed with start points by the user. ETAK depends on the driver. The system turns on it being instructed and updated correctly and one would not expect otherwise.

Now to a most important point not covered by publicity. It does not take long to run off one cassette into the next. What do you do if your destination is on another cassette? Do you programm your route to a suitable point on the edge of your present cassette? What instructions should you give? Then when the first cassette is replaced with the second, having, say, crossed into Oakland, presumably the instructions and memory on the first cassette are fed into the second. One must activate the other – and correctly. Presumably you now enter your final destination on the second cassette. But back to the first cassette, what instructions should it be given before you set off? You cannot enter your final destination, which lies on a second cassette.

There are other problems that are universal in this field, centering on what does the map include and leave out. Are all the minor roads shown? There is a turn on the ground – but it goes into a car park. It that on the map?

Moreover, it must be presumed that the map distance is along the centre line of the road. There can be considerable differences in distance travelled on a six-lane highway or on an urban or city circuit between inner and outer lanes. This applies to many systems reliant on dead reckoning, which are causing other manufacturers and the Transport and Road Research Laboratory in the UK to look for outside agencies.

Yet summing up, notwithstanding the questions posed, clearly the system has a great deal to offer the cross-urban area motorist who cannot drive with a street guide or map in his hand. Now he has a visual display which can be enlarged for detail, changing as he goes along. He may have a problem of bright sunlight affecting the visibility of the display – hence the move by certain manufacturers to synthesize instructions as well.

Finally, to use the system you will have to be a good map reader and navigator. Someone, to whom a map makes no sense at all and who cannot follow a route easily, may do a little better by using the system but not all that much.

Demonstrations of a system have impressed visitors, but then so have demonstrations of equipment by other manufacturers. They usually do. General Motors will be installing ETAK in its more expensive range.

One question that must arise in any urban inner city system is how the computer recognises one-way streets. If it directs the driver wrongly and leads to an accident, can there be a claim for consequential liability? This certainly raises problems in route decision and following. It is one question that EVA (Blaupunkt), in Germany, seeks to answer among others.

EVA (Blaupunkt/Bosch)

German companies have also focused on the use of electronic guidance systems to take motorists through unfamiliar urban areas and towns. Urban and city areas become difficult with a confusion of roads and signs, roundabouts and diversions.

EVA (an acronym of Elektronischer Verkehrslotse für Auto-fahrer – electronic traffic pilot for car drivers) is specifically designed to guide motorists in built-up areas. This demands great accuracy as it has to cope with city centres where crossroads can be as close as 5m apart and any system must be able to distinguish between one and another.

EVA relies on two navigational aid systems:

(i) a system to establish the car's location
(ii) an urban or town road plan in minute detail, stored in the computer, located on the dashboard, that works out the route and monitors it as it is followed.

As with systems already described, changes in direction are given by sensors on the non-driving wheels. Differences in distance travelled will give direction.

To be precise *the system turns on an outside agency to establish position*, eg coils under the road or on beacons, so that there is a constant cross-check on the car's position – which will be constantly updated in relation to the road plan.

When a car turns a corner the system registers the fact. The driver need not keep to a prescribed route. A traffic diversion may force him to seek an alternative and the system will switch to another route. The manufacturer claims that the system does not necessarily choose the shortest distance but takes account of one-way streets and other factors.

In Germany, Siemens, in collaboration with Volkswagen, have produced the AUTO-SCOUT which uses a highly sensitive magnetic compass, both for position and direction finding.

The compass is the size of a matchbox, sensitive to one thousandth of the Earth's magnetic field and, when set horizontally in the vehicle, responds to horizontal waves of the magnetic field. As with any magnetic compass the system is influenced by metal in the car, electrics – internally and externally – and by reinforced concrete structures. Interference within the car can be taken into account by the computer but external interference has to be monitored and offset.

Section 2A: Automatic Vehicle Location Systems

A truck carries a load of gold bars through city streets and urban areas to the airport. Or it could be a car with a VIP – or anyone at risk. It is discreetly marked and has no escort but no chance is taken. At a control room miles away, an operator with a console at his side watches a television-screen-sized colour VDU. The screen shows a digitized map. As the truck moves an arrow on the map moves pointing to the precise place it has reached and travels along with it. The operator can zoom in and enlarge the map so that he can see the truck's location to within 100m, see the road widths, note if the truck is obliged to deviate in any way. If the truck stops or any suspicion is aroused the police can be alerted in seconds.

All this is possible with an AVLS. Fleet operators can watch the movements of their vehicles and cab firms their cars.

The system I shall describe is the VELOTRAC* from Racal Positioning Systems. Other manufacturers, Plessey and ETAK among them, have produced AVLSs. Racal, with experience of Decca navigation going back to 1944, should be able to produce a workable land navigation system. It is really a case of adapting what the company already does in marine and air.

The Racal system uses either LORAN, or its own pulse system Decca Main Chain. The control centre has a polling processor, linked to a display processor and that to a keyboard and VDU. The polling processor links with a modem and the VHF base station. It links the base station with the mobile. The vehicle has a LORAN AVL positioning unit the size of a portable typewriter, a dead reckoning processor, a digital modem interface and a UHF or VHF data transmitter/receiver. Outside, the vehicle has the same short whip antenna as for any radiophone.

As an addition, the vehicle could have a status keyboard to enter short coded messages to control; an emergency button to raise the alarm automatically at control; vehicle display showing location (a Vodaphone cellular telephone may be used instead of a VHF transceiver to link the mobiles to the base).

In the vehicle Racal would use either a LORAN type receiver or a special version of the Decca Main Chain receiver. In either case the receiver is of specialised design such that it has inputs from the vehicle mileometer and from a small fluxgate compass. These inputs are computed to provide a basic dead reckoning track, continuously checked against the position given from the radio input.

---

*In prototype, at time of writing. Police forces resist any use of their VHF systems for any other purpose than direct radio contact between officers in the field and between officers and HQ, ie they would not use their VHF system for an AVLS.

The whole system costs (provisionally) £2,500, US$3,750, to instal.

To begin with, the system works. You can even see where it may go wrong – as in an underpass, with all the metal that throws it for a while – but the system soon corrects itself. It starts with a great advantage. It gives location from the outset, as well as en route. It does not depend on accurate initialisation. For 99% plus of the journey you can track the moving vehicle over an intricate route, even watch the vehicle take a wide curve as it leaves one highway for another.

As with any vehicle navigation system it uses a digitized map. Before operation, the vehicle compass deviations are measured and calibrations are adjusted using the radio navigation system.

In the normal way the grid squares giving Eastings/Northings on the display at control are 2km, but they can be instantly enlarged to 1km, 0.5km and so on down to 100m. This bringing up of area highlights the problem of map accuracy. The location as indicated by the arrow, may be right, but may not appear so if the road was slightly out on the map.

It is doubtful whether police forces would use such a system.[*] But it would appear attractive and of use to security firms and fleet operators. The principle, though, has a wider application. For it will give anyone driving an accurate location if linked, through phone and a modem, to control. It also shows that Racal, which has looked hard at vehicle navigation systems, has decided that its system must have an outside agency and not rely on compass, sensors and dead reckoning.

Section 3: Digitizing

NB I am indebted to Lt. Col. Ben Burrows, writer of the MOD manual, for information in this and the next section.

Digital Mapping
Without digitized maps so much of this Part 8, on the new technology, could not have been written. It would not have happened. The technological breakthrough, perhaps unglamorous and unpublicised, that has facilitated hand and in-car navigation systems is the ability to transform the data on the map to a form that a computer can handle.

There are two basic methods of digitizing:

(i) the raster data system, where the entire area is scanned with a recording head, moving in straight lines a very small distance apart. The area is divided into a matrix of cells. Each cell will have associated values that describe the territory enclosed by the cell. The computer, linked to a VDU, gives a map display as seen on television in weather forecasts. It gives a similar picture to that of a medical body scan

(ii) the vector** system, involves a **selectivity**, where individual lines are followed with a recording head or cursor. The digitized maps in systems described in this section of Part 8 are vector based. The process is carried out manually or semi-automatically. Vector mapping demands instructions, viz the selection of features to be mapped.

As a result, there is flexibility; maps can be reduced and enlarged instantly; repetitive tasks can be carried out at speed. This ensures constant accuracy and can employ a third dimension, height, the z co-ordinate and so construct a model giving the terrain surface. I have already referred to the use of such a three-

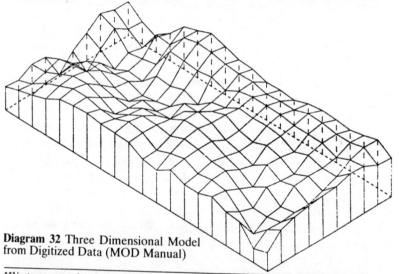

Diagram 32 Three Dimensional Model from Digitized Data (MOD Manual)

**Vector contour data is transformed into a mesh or matrix of points having x, y and z co-ordinates representing corresponding points on the surface of the terrain, producing terrain elevation files, known collectively as Digital Terrain Elevation Data (DTED). This may be supplemented by feature files which contain information relating to the features on the surface of the terrain, known collectively as Digital Feature Analysis Data (DFAD). Features may be selected and related to the terrain to meet specific requirements; thus the road network may be displayed, or objects having radar reflectance characteristics may be selected. Because the information is stored in digital form and can be selectively retrieved, significantly more information may be assembled than would be possible to depict on a conventional map.

Additionally, digital terrain models of selected areas may be rotated by computer so that the view of the terrain may be varied to meet the observer's requirements.

Diagram 33 Simulated View Stanley Airfield (MOD Manual)

dimensional model to solve quickly problems of intervisibility, given all the provisos. The diagram shows a model constructed from digitized map data.

Diagram 33 shows a simulated view of Stanley Airfield in the Falkland Islands from the South East. The vertical exaggeration is ×4.5.

Digitizing has yet another plus. A map can be brought up-to-date by a press of a button, taking out the old and printing the new. Formerly corrections were a lengthy process.

In the USA, the Geological Survey digitizes maps. However ETAK is developing its own digital map data base covering the USA and one quarter of the roads in metropolitan areas have been mapped. The Census Bureau DIME file gives digital co-ordinates of street names, addresses and other data useful in taking the census, which ETAK uses as a prime source of urban data. For the maps, co-ordinates are taken from either the Geological Survey topographical maps, or from aerial photographs.

As regards costs and the digitizing of maps; the hardware comprising a mini-computer, a high resolution graphics terminal and a digitizing tablet and a plotter would start at £100,000 (US$150,000). The associated software would begin at £20,000 (US$30,000). These are prices of the mid 1980s. The purchase price of digitized maps from the Ordnance Survey in Britain or the Geological Survey in the United States can be obtained on request, but is not all that expensive. Large scale digitized maps are used especially in boundary definition and similar urban problems.

TACIPRINT

Generals allege that battles are fought at the four corners of adjacent maps. The military have produced an answer – TACIPRINT, which may change map production and usage in the decades ahead.

TACIPRINT can join those four corners into a new map, can mark overprints, such as military dispositions, on maps within half to one hour – and print forty copies in a minute. The system began with the need for an accurate overprint of minefield location.

The complete TACIPRINT unit fits into the back of a four-ton truck. It comprises:

(i) a rotaprint RA 2S lithographic printing press
(ii) a Hitherm dyeline printer
(iii) an Agfa Gevaert D 2666 4 bath processing unit
(iv) a Berkey Ascor exposing frame
(v) a Littlejohn light table
(vi) a hinged sink with showerhead water supply.

The unit can be taken anywhere, though it demands reasonably level ground.

TACIPRINT does not enlarge or reduce. It reproduces the map and tracings presented to it at the same size. The unit carries map reproduction material at 1:250,000; 1:100,000; and 1:50,000 scales.

Section 4: New Developments and Gyro
The Transport Researcher's Auto-guide

At the time of writing, television and the press have announced yet another end to the need for a map – at least in city and urban areas – with the vision of a world where drivers will be guided through city streets by a voice from the dashboard.

The publicity emanates from a project by the TRRL (Transport and Road Research Laboratory) a government agency in the UK, which has developed a system called AUTOGUIDE. Any project from the TRRL has to be taken seriously as its work is based on *continuous* research by scientists, who can take a critical view of other systems and possibilities. AUTOGUIDE's first stage project – really a test trial – envisages 700 beacon sites near traffic junctions in the Greater London area, within the M25 road circuit. These will emit signals that, fed into a computerized unit in a vehicle, would instruct the driver to turn left onto the A3 or take the street ahead on the A217. The system tailors its recommended route according to the vehicle type, eg it may not give the same route for a heavy truck as for a car, and also it changes the route according to the time of day, so as to avoid possible bottlenecks. This timing is very clever indeed, as it will work out, for instance, the traffic situation which the vehicle will encounter an hour or more ahead en route to its destination. At 7am, when the vehicle sets off, all roads may be clear but the computer works out that later in the journey the possible route would be crowded.

Moreover, if vehicles have gone through a checkpoint and taken too long to a later point, so indicating a hold-up, the system will re-route following traffic.

The TRRL has developed AUTOGUIDE from a system called NAVIGATOR, developed by Lucas Ltd under contract to the agency, which has its own electronic map representation and gives route directions to the driver based on the distance travelled from the last junction. AUTOGUIDE was also developed from ROUTE-TEL, the computerization of route guidance, where the TRRL has investigated the problems of shortest versus fastest routes.

AUTOGUIDE is a step up from British Telecom's PINPOINT, a network of short range radio beacons which enable fitted vehicles to transmit their locations and identities back to a control centre.

Significantly, there is no use of dead reckoning, unlike the German counterpart ALI-SCOUT, developed in Berlin by a consortium of German companies, that combines the use of roadside beacons with a dead reckoning device in the unit, so that the unit itself can give directional guidance even when no information is available from the beacon system. This enables ALI-SCOUT to use fewer beacons. ALI-SCOUT steps up on car navigation systems which turn on compass and dead reckoning, by using an outside agency, viz roadside beacons.

The TRRL claims that its system would save £100 million per year in wasted vehicle time and fuel and even accidents, reducing the average journey time by around 10%. All the driver has to do is to feed in his destination and then the unit guides him either on a visual display or by a voice synthesizer. So far so good!

The problem – again, at the time of writing – is that the TRRL is looking for an organisation to invest £150–200 million (US$225–300 million) and recover the costs and even to make a profit by charging users around £150 (US$225) for the unit in their vehicles.

The TRRL is confident of finding a company to do this. However, this is still a test project, and the scientists agree with the point I have made to them, that the system depends on the user *recognising* the turn to which he is directed – a universal problem with or without the technology. If the system says A23, does the driver know which road is the A23 at the junction or roundabout? That depends on the clarity and positioning of the road signs and the position of a driver in the traffic – and on the time of day. It may be very difficult to get into the right lane and take the right route if other lines of traffic have to be crossed in the last seconds. How well then can the system *anticipate* instructions? Such instructions given from, say, 100m ahead may have to say more than just 'turn left' or 'right' or 'straight ahead at the road junction'. Motoring organisations in Britain have continually criticised road signs, particularly in urban areas, and this must present a problem to the users of such a system.

As said before in this book, with any system, those who know navigation well will profit, and those who are uncertain may not do so well.

The TRRL claims the system will be continuously updated, minute by minute; processing road information from police, motoring organisations, local authorities and even the weather people. Now this is important, for computerized navigation systems described in this book turn on the map being up to the minute. One buys a cassette but how soon will that cassette be out of date? What happens if the cassette has a one-way system even a day out of date? I referred earlier to the question of consequential liability if an accident results. How far has this question been considered?

Meanwhile, a considered reflection on all the new technology! Reacting to the publicity for the electronic systems, the Director General of the British Automobile Association, speaking at a world conference, criticised the concept of technology taking over navigation and driving. He criticised especially the disturbing prospect of computers organising traffic at speed only a few yards apart – allegedly to improve traffic flow. The AA Director General, in contrast, emphasised the importance of *human judgement*; the person at the wheel. I agree. For, as I said earlier, notwithstanding all the technology scientists can develop, *navigation and map reading depend on the navigator* – a member of homo sapiens. Even when armed with all the computerized technology, there is no substitute for the human brain.

Navigation – and hence map reading – becomes an exercise in human behaviour.

Ironically a great tribute to the ability of the human brain to cope with complexities comes from those working on a system of autonomous vehicles, at the behest of the military. An autonomous vehicle can perform a series of operations without a driver, just by reacting to situations as it observes them and feeds back the information. Hence it is very useful in dangerous situations. But to design the built-in computer that will recognise what is happening and act accordingly, the scientists studied the way the human brain operates; how it perceives and instructs. They then build a computer to do likewise, to read both the country and the maps and so programme its movements.

Gyro Instruments

The military are most concerned to have a system that does not depend on an outside agency, such as satellite or radio beacons or a remote operator, where communication can be intercepted or falsified.

It is for this reason also that the military have long used and studied self-contained inertial guidance systems. So to a clever instrument of inertial navigation – compact, small; costing US$45,000 – a North-seeking gyro. It is based on the rotation of the Earth. It gives *true north* wherever you are. It is already used by United States and British Forces and needs the briefest training to operate.

So you can straightway set out map on the lines of longitude and latitude. Unlike a magnetic compass no external forces will deflect it. It will give true North. Unlike some of the car guidance projects, it has been little publicised; it works. It follows the development and use of Gyro instruments.

Introduction*

1 The characteristic of a spinning mass, or spinner, is that it resists any disturbing force which seeks to change the direction of its axis of rotation. A sensor may therefore be arranged to detect this resistance and display it as either digital or analogue information.

---

*From a memorandum of Lt. Col. Ben Burrows.

If a spinner is suitably mounted and set in a given direction it can be used to detect and measure changes in direction, *hence the gyro-compass*.

2 Gyro-compasses in various forms have been available for more than half a century but until recently their bulk, weight and complication have placed severe limitations on their use. Gyro-compasses must be set to point to true North; North-seeking gyro-instruments align themselves with true North and therefore it is not necessary to align them first to true North.

3 In a totally inert space the spin axis of any gyroscope will maintain a constant direction, but the Earth spinning on its axis can be regarded as a gyroscope and therefore any gyroscope on the Earth's surface is itself influenced by the spinning Earth. If the spinner of a gyroscope is arranged so that its axis is in a horizontal plane, and if it is suspended so that it can rotate only about the local vertical, the rotational forces created by the Earth will urge the axis of the *gyroscope to align itself with the horizontal component of the Earth's rotation and hence the local meridian and thus point to true North*.

4 The frame carrying the spinner may be suspended on a wire which acts as a plumb-line and automatically identifies the local vertical, or it may be contained in a frame which is levelled by spirit bubbles. The whole assembly is mounted on or under a theodolite, which can then be related to the direction of the spinner's axis and hence to the direction of true North. All other directions may then be related to true North in terms of true bearings. Accuracies in the order of ± 0.2m or better may be obtained.

5 It will be evident that power is required to drive the spinner and that the whole arrangement must be very delicately balanced. In order to keep dimensions within manageable limits, the spinner must be driven at very high speed, in the order of 25,000rpm, and it must be given time to align itself in the meridian.

6 *North-seeking gyroscopic instruments are most effective in low latitudes where the spin axis is almost parallel to the Earth's axis*; they become progressively less effective with increase of latitude. There are several types of gyrotheodolites which differ in detail, but all of which operate on the same principle. The Precision Indicator of the Meridian (PIM) has been in use for many years and one of the more recent additions to the range is the Wild GAK 1.

'THE LAST WORD': LASER VIDEO DISC

The *last word* to the final section on the new technology can never truly be the 'last word'. Just that I must draw a line across my copy to get it to the printer whilst too aware of continuous research and developments.

Yet an impressive 'last word'. Nine hundred years after William the Conqueror's *Domesday Book*, listing details of every habitation in England, comes a new Domesday record, this time on a laser video disc. This disc comprises more than 5,000 places. Operate the right control and on the VDU you can zoom into a map of the remotest place and then, near miraculous, another control and see a picture of the place itself. Here is an answer to the problem with which this book began, viz you have a map, can you visualise what you will see on the ground? The new technology has the answer. The applications are endless and, quite frankly, if I had not seen it in operation I would find it hard to believe.

Needless to say laser discs will be restricted by the cost, not that of producing a disc – around two thousand dollars – but of getting the data and art-work. For London alone the estimated cost would exceed a million dollars to cover the near endless work of navigators going up and down each street, recording information and taking pictures, to tie up with the map information. The Domesday Disc which I have just described was made possible by grants from charities and foundations.

Technology advances. DATA TRAK, a new navigation system will cover Britain, devised by a consortium, the setting up of beacons to rival British Telecom and the Road Research Laboratory Auto-Guide. Four beacons, giving six base lines, cover London. The system is designed mainly to enable the tracking of vehicles by a central control, an AVLS. It could be used for in-car systems. (DATA TRAK, operated by Wimpey and Securicor, plans beacons throughout Britain, to give national coverage – reporting by Securicor VHF.)

The situation will become even more interesting if Decca were also used for land navigation.

Does it mean that a map is no longer needed? Or the ability to study a map? Or to find the way? Not at all! The map is the source material for the disc and the new technology. You still have to learn how to use the information – still have to learn how to find your way.

Appendix A
Exercises 1–11

Exercise 1

Choose a point 20km (12½ miles) away from your home, *not on a direct route from where you are*. Call the place point 'A'. A railway station, maybe, or an important road junction. Now write a simple instruction to a friend visiting you for the first time on how to get to your home.

Rules: 1 Select prominent or distinctive places en route that your friend will *recognise* – and not confuse with anywhere else. They are called *landmarks*, the basis of all route finding.

2 Write the directions from one place to another, North, East, South and so on – **direction**.

3 Write in the distances from point to point – **distance**; kilometres, miles.

These are the three elements of all route planning and following.

Dont's: no counting of turnings, no lefts and rights. Be wary of such points en route as a phone booth or letterbox. There may be others nearby to confuse.

Do's: write in such helpful information as the route going downhill or uphill and note how useful a landmark is the brow of a hill from where you have to turn *east* into a minor road, or where you turn having reached the bottom of a hill.

Don't try to be too clever with an involved route. Do simplify. If need be take a little longer but have less chance of going wrong.

NB **Direction:** although in practice you move left and right such instructions have a serious drawback. It all depends on which way you face. Hence, in this exercise begin thinking and working by points of the compass.

Distance: the world is becoming metric. In Britain maps are in both miles and kilometres, so you need to be able to operate in both measures.

Exercise 2

Now mark up your route in Exercise 1 **in time** as well as distance. How long from point to point at a reasonable speed in a car; give a margin either way, eg 10 minutes plus or minus 1 minute from the railway station to the Pig & Whistle.

Imagine you are on a bicycle and give times accordingly.

Exercise 3

Draw a sketch map of the route you took in Exercises 1 and 2. Use a full page of your sketch pad.

Before you draw anything put in a line pointing to true North.

Mark in first your start and finishing points to give yourself the greatest distance in between. Then with your ruler calculate the scale you are going to work to, eg 20km to '*x*' centimetres.

Convert your distances en route to centimetres on your sketch map. Then put in the intermediate places.

Now write in the roads and junctions on the actual route to be traversed with landmarks and other features.*

Exercise 4

Follow-up to exercises 1 and 2

Take a colleague in your car and go over the route you have devised.

(i) let your colleague read from your instructions at the appropriate places and times and see how he works it out.
(ii) get your colleague to check the distances (from your mileage recorder on the car) and times and record them in the notebook. Compare with your original version.

Exercise 5

Direction

On a sheet of a sketch pad, mark a cross in the centre to show the location of your home. Draw a line parallel with the left hand edge

---

*Now buy an Ordnance Survey map scale 1:50,000 of your home area. **Compare**! See how your friend would have got on from the map. Note what the map has not shown or where it is particularly helpful.

of the sheet to indicate North. Then, from the centre cross, draw lines to show the direction of

(i) where you work or study
(ii) the railway station
(iii) the nearest airport
(iv) the nearest pub or bar
(v) two churches

Now repeat the exercise on another sheet of your sketch pad. This time from your place of work or study. Draw lines *from there* to places (ii) to (v) and to your home.

Exercise 6

Conventional Signs
Take a 1:50,000 map of an area you do not know too well but which is not too far away. Select two points 20km apart *not* joined by a motorway or main trunk road; broken country in between.

Trace a route from one point to the other. Describe and record it by means of the conventional signs on the map in a notebook.

Now go over that route on the ground and compare your notes with what you see. Repeat for a locality with a different set of features.

Exercise 7

Find a river valley running into the hills. Stand at a vantage point lower down where you can see the slopes of the hills on either side of the valley as it goes into the hills.

1 On your sketch pad draw three or four form lines to convey the slopes you can see on either side – miniature country. Then indicate the highest points on your sketch pad.
2 Now draw in where the roads run – and railways if there.
3 Compare now the area on a 1:25,000 or 1:50,000 map. On tracing paper go over contours at 200ft (61m) and 400ft (122m) and so on at these intervals, as suggested in the text on shape of country.
4 Compare the trace with your sketch of miniature country.

Exercise 8

This exercise can teach you a great deal about route finding on wheels – and about yourself, as regards your problems in navigation. You learn what to look for when locating the route; the landmarks, reference points and something about the layout of road systems aside from what you remember well when driving. What do you see and recognise and remember? Where do you go wrong? *Note*: begin the exercise *without* consulting a map. Route finding comes first, then you appreciate what the map can do for you. But to get on your way you need a notebook, an eye for detail and a flask of tea!

Select a place about 120km (75 miles) away, which you may have visited or gone through in the past. It could be a place you visit occasionally. Now set off to drive there, without a map, but trying a different route to the one you have taken; just head in the right direction. At the outset you may be on a road you have taken before but as soon as possible get on unfamiliar roads.

Plan to stop three or four times on the way. At each stop record in the notebook:

(a) the route taken so far, with distances
(b) how you would identify the route if you had to describe it to others
(c) any landmarks that locate or anticipate a turn point
(d) related to (c) landmarks that will help on the return route
(e) any problems? Where can one go wrong?

Try to get to your destination without having to ask anyone the way.

At your destination plan the return journey over the same route. Write down the points that guide you.

Having completed the out and home journey *now* follow the route you have taken on the map – first on a 1:250,000 or similar scale and then on 1:50,000.

Which features on the map guide you best? Any vital information you recorded *not* on the map? What does the map include? What does it leave out?

Now compile your own prompt cards, memory aids – listing places, landmarks, distance, road information and any other detail on the card or cards to guide you out and home.

Exercise 9

Choose a point 100km (62½ miles) away from your home, which can be reached partly by motorway. Plan the route to that point on a 1:200,000 or 1:250,000 scale map, using the motorway. **Estimate** time of arrival. Now plan the return route on the older highways on a 1:50,000 map. Check that route on a smaller scale 1:200,000 and note the effect of scale.

Now follow your plan – out by the motorway and back by the other roads. You may be able to do so on a business trip or day out for pleasure.

Record in a notebook:

(i) time and mileometer reading at start
(ii) same readings at furthest point
(iii) readings on return
(iv) where hold-ups occur on way out and return
(v) any difficulties and special points en route
(vi) sum up – pluses and minuses of the two routes.

(For use of memory prompt card in conjunction with this exercise – see Part 4).

Exercise 10

Judgement of time and distance

How good is your judgement of time and distance? Many problems stem from the difficulty to adapt to the rate of change of scenery in relation to the width of the highway. A wider road and the surroundings seem to 'move' more slowly – hence motorway crashes, where judgement is most impaired by road width. You need to train those faculties, sense of time, speed and distance. There is not magic in this; just practice!

(i) *the conditions permitting* – traffic free – drive 2km approximately at 48kph (30mph)
   (a) on a narrower road
   (b) on a wider road
   (c) on a very wide road

The distance identified by measurement on a 1 to 10,000 map from one marker to another easily recognised may be over the 2km distance when looking for an identifiable point.

(ii) repeat, *without* looking at speedometer but with a passenger instead to alert you when you go over the speed.

(iii) try a variation on a sound surface and on a poorer one, especially (a) and (b).

(iv) now step up to 72kph (45mph) and repeat the exercise.

(v) repeat for 88kph (55mph) on a wider road

(vi) at end of 2km exercise estimate the time taken and check against a passenger's stop watch.

(vii) now, on different roads – narrower, wide and wider – drive at 48kph (30mph) and signal to your passenger when you have gone past an identifiable point at approximately 2km and 3km. Check on a 1 to 10,000 map.

(viii) Repeat (vii) at 73kph on 'other' roads and on another wider road at 88kph.

Try timing yourself over 2km distance on the flat whilst bicycling – get the feel of the 3-minute km and then 2 minute 30 secs km.

Exercise 11

Variation on Card Prompt

Obtain a Michelin 1 to 200,000, No. 230 Bretagne (Brittany) map. Devise your own route cards from Avranches, North East of the map, round Rennes to Concarneau to the South West. Split the route at Plöermel, making 2 cards.

Try this system – left to right across the card –

(i) direction

(ii) distance

(iii) place name, abbreviated

(iv) strip road diagram with turnings off

(v) warning signs where one might go wrong, eg at Hennerbrant making sure to pick up Quimperle road marked 4 on map.

Note, in France as elsewhere ring roads round major cities/ towns, e.g. Rennes. On the approach these ring roads are usually marked 'Toutes diréctions' – the only problem is getting off these circuits at the 'diréction' one wants!

Note the scenic stretch West of Baud. There are many such stretches on this route; the road edged with green, indicating that it overlooks areas with fine views, hills, rivers, lake or sea views. This tells about the road itself; it will certainly *not* be a six-lane highway.

Memo on Instruction

This book began from the instruction of personnel of varying ability and interest in active service conditions. No signposts; reliance on one's own resources, certainly little chance to ask or dive into a phone box. If one is lost, tactical considerations, often unsafe to observe from a place with a good view; navigation at night, silent and no lights; above all, mistakes could prove serious. Hence the accent in this book on warnings against what may go wrong, all based on experience – and it has had to be a repeated experience to be included.

On the other hand, instruction must be positive. *What to do?* This guards against mistakes. Sometimes I accent what *not* to do, such as not to plan routes by counting turnings or planning directions in terms of left and right. *They are out.* But an alternative must be provided. Plan by landmarks, use North, South, East and West, bearings and distance. When you drive you may think left and right and instruct someone to do so but you do not plan that way on the map.

Approach/Method

This is a subject that cannot be taught by lectures and reading. To master map reading and navigation you must *participate* from the outset. The preceding exercises are designed to help you teach yourself through practical activity, relevant to sections of the subject. The preceding exercises could well form the framework of an instruction course.

However, aside from the exercises, here are the general principles in the instruction of the subject.

(a) from the outset look at the countryside, at what the map depicts, before getting down to maps. Observe systematically the types of country, sketch what you see, chart where you have been, construct models. Discuss!

(b) then to the map. The map is a *tool* in navigation but, as I stated at the outset, the best map reader is the one who can navigate best without a map, who needs the map least. The best navigator soon learns the detail needed to be grasped from the map – the details to guide him.

(c) the student may get engrossed in the refinements of the map and all the attendant detail – though this detail may be lost when in the middle of a desert or a highway, tangled up from a succession of roundabouts, diversions – and misleading signs!

(d) the *use* of a map is the main concern, so master the detail needed for a purpose – to find the way or if static to appreciate an area of ground. It is the carrying out of a particular job that gives the interest in using the map – the interest that helps one learn and retain information.

(e) all methods of instruction must foster this interest. *Learning through activity* makes it pleasurable. The activity must cultivate observation, develop a sense of country, awareness of direction, judgement of distance and time and thus develop memory for landmarks and routes and road systems.

(f) orienteering is activity, competitive and fun and so aids learning. But this comes at a later stage when you know maps. It is a sport and should be regarded as such and be included in advanced map reading. How far it helps in certain problems of route finding – especially on wheels or tracks – is another question.

Syllabuses

Clearly any programme must be adapted to ability and needs. However:

(i) start *outdoors* before looking at a map; sketch, make notes, describe what you can see and the routes out and back. Then go to reference libraries to establish the underlying geology that determines the land forms you have seen.

(ii) construct your own map and a model; compare them with a printed map of differing scales. The map now means something.

(iii) outdoors again, route finding, without a map and then with.

(iv) now the details on the map, the signs, contours, the way the map represents any symbols, the reality on the ground.

(v) compass, protractor, bearings – tedious, maybe, but no option – sun and stars. Then outdoors on direction exercises.

(vi) *group sessions on problems and techniques of route finding. How do individuals cope? Any special methods of their own? What would the group do if lost? How to cope on the highway, the motorway exits and interchanges.

(vii) memory; a subject on its own. Memory prompts and route cards.

(viii) special situations, the desert and mountains – and urban areas that look alike and what happens when you get off the main highway.

(ix) sessions on field sketching.

(x) more on road route diagrams, directional framework, time and distance exercises.

(xi) orienteering exercise.

(xii) revision: landmarks, identification of routes, what are observed and more easily memorised. Anticipatory landmarks. Shape of country and layout of manmade features that result from the shape of country.

---

*Best start a programme with this item and then come back to it again at this stage.

Appendix B

On Memory and Learning

Memory plays a major role in map reading and navigation. The techniques put forward derive from the difficulty, indeed, the impossibility, of travelling and studying a map at the same time.

By the time you set out you need to be armed with a picture, however sketchy, of the territory you are to traverse and have a route outline in your head.

There are books on memory. One, *Speed Memory* by Tony Buzan (David & Charles), lists systems whereby you can link what you need to retain with numbers, initials and words that you should find easier to recall. Association with the familiar aids memory – and with humour or an everyday phrase. Retain a catch phrase, such as 'right up', to guide you in reference numbers.

For Route Cards I have suggested memorising the initials of the key places en route. Do they form a word? Motorway exits in Britain are numbered. A key number or numbers can be remembered and if you have to leave at exit 6, then as you pass exit 5 or 7 (depending on the direction of travel) look out for the turn you need.

It is claimed that repetition rehearsal, especially verbal, aids memory. Not all evidence supports this, but it may work for some and even if others think you are odd, why not repeat aloud, or even sing, the places and landmarks that define your route. Landmarks form the skeleton of the route – the places where you turn, the points, too, where you can go wrong. Fortunately in the UK, so often a pub marks a crossroad or junction. Unfortunately, the maps do not show them; yet the names can so effectively identify a route. I remember the sequence used on a route through the lanes to avoid a busy highway, which reads: 'The Seven Stars', 'The Fox Revived', 'The Rising Sun' and so on.

Here memory is aided by interest, an important factor. A man in a bar remembers not only the winner of the 1921 Derby, but the second and third and the sires and dams of the three horses. Yet at school he forgot instantly, if he ever knew, the battles of the Wars of the Roses, or the children of Queen Victoria. History sent him to sleep. *Horses are his hobby.* Here his memory is reinforced by two factors:

(i) his hobby is *self taught* – and what you teach yourself is far more likely to be remembered

(ii) you are not the first to whom he has repeated his gems of information – maybe for a bet, another stimulant to thought, as are many games. So he feels important, acquiring the status of an expert.

It can be reasonably predicted, too, that although he failed in school arithmetic, he can calculate in a flash the returns on his bets at the bookmakers. This produces its instant reward. He knows if he is being paid out correctly.

The points I have made apply to the teaching of the subject as well as its use. A major task is to foster memory of maps and country. Can you recognise the country and its features from the map and retain that knowledge?

Memory is aided by:

(i) **systematic** study of the map: a drill, a **sequence**, first water, then highest points and so on.

(ii) **simplifying** both the information on the map and the instructions from it to retain a handful of major landmarks and directions. Hence my disagreement with those orienteering maps that overelaborate detail.

(iii) sketch country to retain information; draw simple route diagrams; **set yourself a task**, that will aid your memory. In this task you can devise a route and country shorthand; a sign for a major hill; exclamation mark for a point where you must look out, make a turn; a symbol for a landmark.

(iv) at all stages sharpen your observation! Look at an area of countryside. Turn away and write down the details. Sketch what you have seen. Look again and check – train your eyesight. (Incidentally, work conscientiously through the exercises in this book.)

(v) repeat point (iv) with a map. Follow a route through, turn the map over – sketch the route and add all the information you have seen – *check* what you have done.

Can you associate the information needed to retain the landmarks with the initials of words, or incorporate them into a rhyme or a catchy tune?

Useful habits help the memory. Once outdoors, if the sun is shining, fix North and South,* just as a routine and repeat later as the time elapses, especially while you are on the move. At night in the same way look for the North Pole Star and the constellations in

---

*For method see Part 3

the sky that point to it when you leave home – or even when stepping out of a car when parking it. This activity heightens your awareness of directions. (See Part 3: Section 5.)

To operate in an area, memorise the directions of main features; a river, railway or hill system. Memorise, too, the main distances. As with any faculty, memory thrives on use. Memory also aids confidence. Confidence, but not obstinacy, reduces the chances of being lost. Fear of getting lost may well lead to its happening, a point made in Part 7.

Finally, an army custom. Wherever you go, look back *when you can*, to fix the return route in your head. The world can look different in reverse and is not always so easily recognisable.

Appendix C

Field Sketching and Panorama

Notes on this subject
Not only does field sketching prove invaluable for reinforcing information, but the act of making your own sketch maps teaches you map reading. A picture can convey more than words.

You must develop a rapid method of field sketching, without too much sacrifice of accuracy.

Field Sketching by Bearings
This method can best be explained by means of an example. Imagine that you have to survey the slopes of the West side of a river. You are on the Eastern bank. Select two points from which to make your observations. From each viewpoint draw a picture of what you can see, indicating all the important features, showing heights by rough form lines, and estimating the distances to the various features. Also record in your notebook the bearings on the principal objects in the landscape, marking in these points carefully in on the sketch you draw.

From each viewpoint take bearings on the same features. Measure accurately (the pacing method is sufficiently accurate) the distance between the two bases.

Then go back to start on your sketch map as follows:

1 Estimate the largest distance on your sketch, and on the basis of this decide on the scale. The usual aim is to make a sketch map neatly fill your sheet of paper.
2 Draw in the base line, ie the viewpoints.
3 Plot in all the bearings you have recorded from these two viewpoints.
4 By means of your drawings in the field complete the sketch.
5 Write in, either on the map itself, or in the margins, all useful information, eg **Roads** : surface, width, ditches, drainage, hedges, fences, obstacles, cuttings, etc, state of repair and so on for **bridges : railways : rivers : habitations/buildings**. As regards rivers – indicate by an arrow the direction of flow and mark in the estimated speed, depth and width. Note too, the **Vegetation:** trees, bushes, undergrowth, grasses, crops.
6 Represent the scale in the three ways as described in Part 2.
7 Insert the direction of North – it is customary to set a map so that the top points away from you. Therefore you must insert an arrow indicating magnetic North – this is the best North for sketch maps.
8 Write where the ground was surveyed from, the state of visibility, the date, and the signature of the map maker.

Field Sketching from an Enlargement

If you want to make a detailed study of a certain area, for a definite objective, you can survey the country as described, but insert the information on a previously prepared enlargement from a printed map.

The best method of enlargement is the 'Union Jack method'. The area to be enlarged on the original map is bounded off by the four sides of a rectangle with the diagonals and half way lines inserted. This 'Union Jack' is then reproduced to the size wanted on the final sketch. All the features from the original map are then copied in, with their distances from the framework of the 'Union Jack' enlarged in proportion.

The information recorded in the field can then be inserted on this enlargement.

Indication of Heights

You should indicate height in your sketch maps. It will be found advantageous to use a combination of hachures and form lines. It is not very easy to estimate accurately contour lines. You can, however, write in the highest point of a certain feature, the number of feet or metres which you have estimated from your observation point.

In field sketching from an enlargement the problem of heights will have been largely solved for you. Here concentrate on minor folds in the ground, not indicated on the map because of the height of the vertical interval.

Finally, panorama sketching is an art in itself and you need to be shown by an instructor. Again work from focal points and baseline in the distance around which to structure your picture. Add advice from a military text book, below. However, as with sketch maps, let me give one basic warning:

In all sketching one is liable to become obsessed by certain features that one regards as important *but then draws out of scale*. You can emphasise important features in other ways, such as a note at the foot of the sketch. You must, though, keep the features in proportion for, of course, the proportion of the sketch turns on your sighting of them. However, when you are working from an enlargement of a map already drawn to scale, that problem should be solved.

Notes on Panorama Sketching

I add advice from a military textbook of many years ago on panorama sketching, clearly based on hard experience.

(i) give yourself time to study the ground carefully, maybe with binoculars, before putting pencil to paper.

(ii) follow the principle of perspective as far as possible. Clearly the further away an object the smaller it appears to be and should be so represented on paper. Parallel lines receding from the observer therefore appear to converge, the ultimate meeting point being called the vanishing point.

(iii) simplicity is essential. No line should be drawn without a definite idea as to what that line represents and its necessity.

(iv) all natural objects, buildings, trees, hedges, roads, should be shown by conventional outlines only. Unnecessary shading must be avoided. Use a light 'hatch' to distinguish wooded areas from fields where necessary. You are not producing a work of art but a sketch of specific value and importance.

(v) a firm continuous line should be used throughout.

(vi) decide on the extent of country you wish to include. You will find that about 30° of arc is a maximum suitable area to draw on a single sheet. If you wish to include more country, then draw two panoramas, subsequently to be stuck together. A simple method of deciding the extent of country of one panorama is to hold a protractor about 27cm (11in) from the eye, to close one eye and consider the section of the country thus blotted out by the protractor to be the area to be sketched.

Now to work!

   (i) fix on the paper all outstanding points in the landscape in their correct relative positions. The horizontal distances in a picture may be obtained by lowering the protractor and noting which graduation on its upper edge coincides with the feature it is desired to plot. The protractor can then be laid on the paper and the position of the feature marked above the graduation noted. Vertical distances should be similarly obtained by turning the protractor with its long side vertical.

  (ii) in all types of country – possibly not in mountains – the vertical scale of a panorama should be exaggerated in relation to the horizontal scale, in order that minor folds of ground may be easily distinguished. A suitable exaggeration is that of 2:1.

 (iii) (a) all outstanding points which might readily be selected as a reference point should be marked, carefully drawn and made to represent their natural appearance if possible. They must be accentuated with an arrow and a line bearing a suitable label and map reference given where possible.

(b) rivers: use a double line with width diminishing as it recedes. To show actual water's edge the line may be slightly waved.

(c) trees should be represented by outline only, whilst woods in the distance should also only be shown in outline. In the foreground the tops of individual trees may be indicated and may also be shaded – the shading becoming less as the distance from the observer increases.

(d) roads should be shown by double continuous line diminishing in width as it recedes.

(e) indicate railways in the distance by a single line, with telegraph poles shown by vertical ticks.

(f) show churches in simple outline and denote whether tower or spire.

(g) as regards towns or villages, use definite rectangular shapes for houses and indicate outstanding buildings and chimneys.

Your finished panorama should be clear and simple. You can clarify details with colour, eg rivers tinted in blue; roofs red; and roads brown.

Finally, obviously you show who has prepared the panorama, who you are, date, time and notes as to the weather conditions.

Appendix D

Desert Navigation: Dead Reckoning Exercise

Task: you are at point 210.220 near wadi 'Z' and have a rendezvous 660km North East at point 253.243. Few landmarks; none you can identify on the map.
Note:

(i) a minimum three-man operation; one to lead, one to navigate and keep the log and a driver. (If need be, who leads also drives.)

(ii) with more than one vehicle in the exercise the navigator should be in the second vehicle checking the compass, situated mid-vehicle and high, away from the engine and wiring. From there he can line up the first vehicle on the bearing and note its progress – for there are no steering marks. On a new bearing you may even have to get someone to walk out 25 paces from the lead vehicle in the required direction – and return – indicating the bearing on which to drive.

The procedure may sound involved but one thing you should not do is drive out on a bearing and hope to find the way, working from memory, given all the diversions you will have to make.

Now Start (see log and diagram at end)

(i) with luck you can keep going on bearing 45° (1600') for 12.5km (enter in log at end of stage).

(ii) a deep wadi and have to turn North; an irregular route along the brink. You cannot record all kinks in the route – beginners tend to overestimate the kinks. At about 5km (log) a track into a wadi and along it for 2km North East and then another track climbing out on a bearing of 70° (log).

(iii) the track takes you 7.5km at 75° and then at last a sighting mark – on a ridge 20km to the North East. Note a distinctive feature on it, drive on bearing of 45° (18km). Soft sand ahead, but then a line of oil drums, a route through a gap in the ridge (log).

(iv) track curves through gap. After 5km stop and estimate point you have reached as in line with your original bearing of 45°. In log, record curve of track as two lines, 2km at 80° and 3km at 15°.

(v) track turns East, bearing 90°, too far off your required bearing. So proceed across desert on 45° for 15km, pick up track on average bearing of 20° for 6km.

(vi) there *stop*, having covered 70km, with diversions from the start. Chart the log on squared paper with a protractor and ruler and reckon that 6km on a bearing of 75° will take you to your rendezvous. A total of 76km for a 60km direct route.

The log will read like this:

LOG

From Pt 210.200   *Date: 5th May, 19–*

Km on vehicle recorder	Bearing	Dist.	Route
14,506	45°	12.5km	Good going
518.5	0°	5 km	Wadi ridge
523.5	45°	2 km	Track to bed of wadi & along
525.5	70°	7.5km	Track
532	45°	18 km	Sighting on ridge mark – across desert
550	80°	2 km	Track through gap in
552	15°	3 km	ridge (est)
555	45°	15 km	Good going
570	75°	6 km	Track
576	20°	6 km	Across desert

Rendezvous 253.243

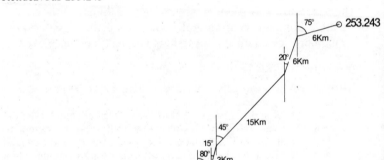
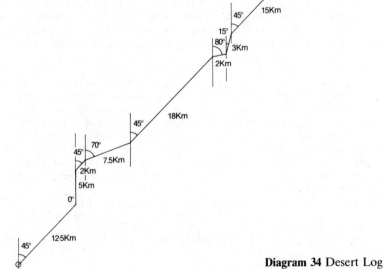

Diagram 34 Desert Log